Resourceful Entrepreneur's Guide to Business in the 21st Century

How to Succeed in Challenging Times

Christine Miller

First published in the United Kingdom by
Porto Publishing June 2011

Porto Publishing
59 The Avenue
Ealing
London
W13 8JR
UK

www.portopublishing.com

A CIP catalogue record for this book is available from the
British Library, London.

Design and Layout by Porto Publishing
Cover Design by Porto Publishing

Paper used in the production of this book complies with the following:
UK - Forest Stewardship Council™ (FSC®) certified.
USA - Sustainable Forestry Initiative® (SFI®) certified

ISBN: 978-1-905930-04-3

PORTO
PUBLISHING
LONDON

Resourceful Entrepreneur's Guide to Business in the 21st Century

How to Succeed in Challenging Times

Christine Miller

To find out more about developing a Resourceful Mind
and becoming a Resourceful Entrepreneur see
www.resourcefulentrepreneur.com.

PORTO
PUBLISHING
LONDON

Contents

No.	Chapters	Page
	Acknowledgements	vi
	Foreword *René Carayol MBE*	vii
	Introduction	1
1	**Prime Your Mind for Success** How to be a Resourceful Entrepreneur *Christine Miller*	7
2	**Delegate Effectively** The Art and Science of Management by Omission *Ricardo Semler*	17
3	**Be Visionary** The 27 Dollar Miracle *Muhammad Yunus*	25
4	**Think Strategically** Think Like an Entrepreneur *Robbie Steinhouse*	33
5	**Learn by Doing** Getting Real: Leaving a Lasting Legacy *Lord Andrew Mawson*	41
6	**Market Organically** Natural Marketing for Lone Rangers *Nicola Cairncross*	51
7	**Succeed on a Shoestring** Developing Success in One of the World's Toughest Environments *Carole Spiers*	59
8	**Remain True to Yourself** The Authentic Article *Toby Buckle*	69

Contents
Cont'd.

No.	Chapters	Page
9	**Attract Clients Naturally** You Don't Need A Personality Transplant To Be Good At Sales *Richard White*	77
10	**Position Yourself Expertly** There's a Book in You – and it will have to come out *Bill O'Hanlon*	83
11	**Plan Well** Three Pitfalls in Goal-Setting - and how to avoid them *Andy Smith*	91
12	**Get Things Done** In Order To Go Faster, First We Must Go Slower *Robyn Pearce*	99
13	**Know Your Numbers** What's Your Financial IQ? Are you Financially Intelligent - or in need of a Money Makeover? *Lisa Wynn*	107
14	**Understand True Wealth** Freeing the Spirit of Money *Steve Nobel*	113
15	**First Things First: Back to the Beginning** *Christine Miller*	119
	Additional Resources	129
	Other Publications	131

Acknowledgements

It's been an exciting journey to bring this First Edition of the 'Ultimate ReSource Guides' to fruition, and for me it represents the fulfilment of a vision I have held for a number of years now. I had always envisaged gathering together collections of the excellent and varied content we publish in ReSource Magazine and presenting it in book form, so I'm thrilled to be writing this at the beginning of a new chapter in our development.

I would like first of all to warmly acknowledge each one of the talented authors and contributors featured here, whose work has such a positive impact in the world, and who it is such a pleasure to include. They exemplify the fact that one person can make a difference, and the importance of being persistent and consistent.

My gratitude goes to Alan Johnson, for his support and diligent input into the design and layout of the book; to Steven Earle and Christophe Poizat for their helpful suggestions and encouragement; to Alex Johnson for his technical insight and expertise, and to the many colleagues and friends both on and offline who have been enthusiastic all along the way.

My thanks go also to René Carayol, MBE, for contributing the Foreword, and for being a champion of entrepreneurs and of inspired excellence in business leadership.

And to all entrepreneurs, everywhere, who are courageous, creative and constantly on the go – keep up the good work, it really is true that the world needs you, and that *we are all entrepreneurs now*.

Foreword

By René Carayol MBE

A few years back the extremely well respected chartered psychologist and strategic advisor Dr Adrian Atkinson delivered a spell binding performance at one of our Inspired Leaders Network event in London on Emotional Intelligence.

It came hot on the heels of an article that was written about him in the Sunday Times in which he categorically stated that "the theory that anyone can become an entrepreneur is absolute nonsense".

In the ongoing "nature vs nurture" debate he pinned his colours securely to the flag of "nature".

In fact, he was so concerned that the wrong type of person shouldn't risk their money and sell everything to become an entrepreneur that he set up a research project with the Prince's Trust to help identify which youngsters should be encouraged into this niche area of the business world, and which should not.

I first met Adrian a few years ago on the set of the hit BBC series 'Mind Of A Millionaire', in which we were both expert witnesses in an attempt to find out if there really was science behind the success of this unique brand of people.

On the first day before we started filming, Adrian and I were sitting in the cafeteria with the 30 'subjects'. All we knew was that half of them were entrepreneurs and that it was Adrian's job to identify these from the rest of the pack using a battery of tests.

He didn't need them.

Within an hour of observing them and engaging in the odd chat, he had identified 14 out of the 15. His knack of spotting the key traits was impeccable; even down to noticing which people were cheating in a quick game of impromptu cards before the hard work began.

"Entrepreneurs have to win - by whatever means necessary"

Come the end of filming he was still just one person out from a 100% accuracy rate. But by then we had done a little digging around and found out that the 15th person was indeed very wealthy but had amassed his fortune over 30 years. Even by his own admission he was a self-made millionaire but by no means an entrepreneur.

He lacked the inherent risk embracing part of their make-up.

So were the rest really all born with the spark, drive, enterprise and total disregard of the stigma of failure?

Dr Atkinson's case was extremely persuasive but some data from the onsite research team's analysis threw up some surprising results that perhaps painted a different picture.

An incredible 49% of entrepreneurs are dyslexic and an even more astounding 59% have come from deprived backgrounds.

And time and again when you speak to these people it is this upbringing of marginalisation or poverty that has, more than anything else, given them the insatiable drive that sets them apart from their peers.

The effect of these formative years is so incredibly powerful that it continues to spur them on throughout their whole life.

So when it comes back to 'nature vs nurture' there is an equally strong case that circumstance can play as pivotal a role as your genes.

Essentially it comes down to desire and the difference between a successful entrepreneur and a failed one is that they never give up.

They keep asking the probing questions, looking for new ways, showing resilience, bouncing back when the chips are down and keeping a steady head in the dizzying highs.

If you take the right mentality and a 'can do' attitude and mix it with commitment and drive, the 'strategy and process' becomes secondary.

It's all about the journey - combining confidence with humility and keeping an open mind to new opportunities. Time and again something unexpected happens that takes you in an entirely new direction that you were least expecting - and it's these opportunities that do not pass entrepreneurs by.

After all, you have to be on the pitch to score a goal.

So let this book be part of YOUR journey; a perfect accompaniment for any entrepreneur and one that sparks ideas and generates momentum.

Just remember, there is never one right answer - and you can never stop learning.

It's time to get out on that pitch.

René Carayol MBE

Introduction

By Christine Miller

This book is dedicated to all big-hearted, open-minded entrepreneurs, who lead businesses large and small, in every part of the world, in honour of your courage, resilience and determination to succeed.

The world needs more entrepreneurs. The word is out everywhere - reality TV programmes are inundated with applicants eager to form partnerships or gain investment funding, and politicians and leaders are telling us that we the people need to be more entrepreneurially minded. Yet there was a time, not too long ago, when the word 'entrepreneur' was pronounced with a degree of distaste in some circles. 'Trade' was definitely not seen as an aspirational sector in which to develop a career!

That perception has radically altered, and in the 21st Century, the world's most successful entrepreneurs are held up as positive role models for young people, and governments encourage entrepreneurship, courting successful business people as advisors on policy and strategy, hoping some of the financial and strategic savvy will rub off. A more collaborative model is emerging, where issues of corporate responsibility and sustainability are of great importance, and transparency is essential.

Resourceful Entrepreneur's Guide to Business in the 21st Century

UK Prime Minister David Cameron recently said:

> *"We won't build the future we want to see in this country if we go back to the bad old days of big government spending, big borrowing and big debt. The recovery we need is a private sector-led recovery, a recovery with* **'Made in Britain'** *stamped all over it. We need to see a country where new businesses are starting up on every street, in every town; where entrepreneurs are everywhere."*

Similar aspirations are expressed in many other parts of the world and business leaders and politicians are very clear in their assertions that it is business that will lift countries and continents back into growth and prosperity, and energise faltering economies.

In those faltering economies, where cutbacks and redundancies in the private sector are now being followed by euphemistically named "efficiencies" in the public sector, many of those employed by central and local government are either finding themselves unemployed or having to re-apply for jobs they have held for years. This means they are entering a competitive world where they need to establish their value, demonstrate their input and impact and justify their existence. In short, they have to sell themselves, and they are ill-equipped to do so, generally lacking the self-promotion and sales skills to present themselves in their best light. Unaware of their assets and resources, when unleashed on the job market, many flounder and do not know what to do for the best.

In another arena, the pressures and demands of corporate life are taking their toll on top talent; many senior executives are pondering their futures, considering if they really want to stay in a competitive, uncooperative cut-throat world where profit is the sole motivator, greed is acceptable, and their work holds little meaning. They then look for more meaningful work, even at a lower rate of pay, or move on to start their own ventures which allow them to collaborate rather than compete and the freedom to pursue their passions and preferences.

Resourceful Entrepreneur's Guide to Business in the 21st Century

Add to this the numbers of school leavers and graduates currently unemployed, and the combination of financial necessity, ethical and personal choice, and demographics means there is a pool of people with enthusiasm and energy who are finding it necessary to develop what we call entrepreneurial skills and attitudes. Whether that means starting their own enterprise or simply being more aware of how to sell themselves, the result is that '**we are all entrepreneurs now'.**

The pitfalls of going it alone, of becoming an entrepreneur, are many, and the failure rate is high. There is limited support available, and funding can be hard to come by these days. In the UK, as many as one in three businesses fail in their first three years[1] - conversely, this means that two thirds do succeed, and many do go on to thrive and prosper.

The advantages of being self-directed, having choice and responsibility, investing your time in something about which you are passionate, which directly impacts your life and benefits your family and community, are many. That is the joy of being your own boss.

Ventures are started by enthusiastic, committed people who want to make a difference. They have a big 'Why' - a vision for their idea, product or service to make a difference, a positive contribution to community and society, and their motives usually extend far beyond monetary success. It's this passion which carries a start-up entrepreneur through the challenges inherent in the whole process.

Such live wires with ideas and energy are unstoppable; and they can also get out of balance and find it very difficult to stay focussed on the activities that need to be planned and performed to make their vision happen. Learning to manage yourself and your mind, directing your thinking and attitude so you are in the optimal state for success, is perfectly possible, but it is not something we are taught in school.

---

1   Source: The Times UK 100 Business Case Studies

It's for this purpose that **The Resourceful Entrepreneur Experience,** of which this book is an important component, has been developed. In **'The Resourceful Entrepreneur's Guide'** we have brought together, just for you, a collection of expert authors whose ideas and guidance can transform your business. The topics cover some of the most important aspects of being a resourceful entrepreneur and successfully building a business to be proud of, which will sustain you whilst it stretches you, and help you become the best you can be.

Whether you are a start-up or an established business, you'll find inspiring guidance and ideas to help you stay on track and think differently about yourself and your venture. The range of leaders and masters in their fields is comprehensive.

You will discover the astonishing transformational power of just one person's determination and persistence: confronted by extreme debt-ridden poverty in his native Bangladesh, Nobel Peace Prize winner **Muhammad Yunus** was driven to start a bank for the poor, and has gone on to transform many lives and bring relief for many millions. **Ricardo Semler,** world famous leadership expert from Brazil, and author of 'Maverick' and 'The Seven Day Weekend', shares his tips for effective delegation and successful collaboration. **Lord Andrew Mawson**, one of the foremost social entrepreneurs in the UK, talks about learning by doing and staying in touch with reality, whilst Robyn Pearce, time and efficiency expert, gives practical solutions for getting more done, faster.

Renowned Business Internet Marketing expert Nicola Cairncross and BBC broadcaster and Communications specialist Carole Spiers talk about different aspects of successful marketing, whilst Richard White describes how sales doesn't require a personality transplant. Bill O'Hanlon guides you to expert status through publishing your own book, Andy Smith gets to grip with goals that work, and Toby Buckle writes on how to stay true to yourself. Time Management expert Robyn Pearce helps you be more efficient. Lisa Wynn and Steve Nobel discuss finances and wealth from different perspectives, giving practical solutions for managing money and a view of the true meaning of wealth and the importance of having the right attitude to being wealthy. It's just like having a panel of mastermind experts on hand to guide you, a rich resource offering a breadth and depth of knowledge rarely found.

You can devour this book all at one sitting, then come back and dip into the chapters when you have a particular need, or simply choose those that appeal to you most, right now, and read and digest their wisdom - then, most importantly - put it into practice.

As an entrepreneur, you are a 'doer' - so read, reflect and then get right into action and make your business and life a true success - become the Ultimate Resourceful Entrepreneur. May your journey be fruitful and enjoyable; we wish you luck, love and prosperity along the way.

Christine Miller

To find out more about developing a Resourceful Mind and becoming a Resourceful Entrepreneur see
www.resourcefulentrepreneur.com.

Christine Miller MA FRSA

Christine is an entrepreneur, author, and results-orientated business and personal growth strategist, who inspires and supports people to create rich, fulfilling, compassionate lives of spirit and heart so that they spend more time doing what they love - and loving what they do.

Christine is renowned for her resourceful creativity and wisdom, her penetrating questions, insights, and ability to provoke transformational thinking and action for organisations and individual coaching and consulting clients worldwide.

As a sought-after expert in Organisational Transformation, Success and Leadership Development, Christine has over 25 years' service in Director level corporate and consulting roles in Marketing and Strategic Planning with major organisations.

Christine is Founder Editor and Publisher of ReSource Magazine, a world famous business and personal growth publication established in 2004, which features valuable broad and deep knowledge on success and transformation.

She has recently interviewed over 50 global leaders from all sectors about creating organisational shifts to a more sustainable, caring and responsible model, the results of which will be available in the form of a book, talks and workshops.

e: learn@resourcefulentrepreneur.com
w: www.resourcefulentrepreneur.com

Chapter 1

Prime Your Mind for Success

How to be a Resourceful Entrepreneur

by Christine Miller

Your Ultimate Resource – Your Resourceful State of Mind

> *"Though an inheritance of acres may be bequeathed,
> an inheritance of knowledge and wisdom cannot. The
> wealthy man may pay others for doing his work for
> him, but it is impossible to get his thinking done for him
> by another or to purchase any kind of self-culture."*
>
> ### S. Smiles

The potential resource inherent in the human race, our wonderful mind and ability to think in advanced ways, is the most neglected asset on the planet. We can, with appropriate training and conditions, harness the power of people and their ability to think, create and act to solve our problems.

At present we don't have those appropriate conditions. We take care to educate people with facts and figures, and then we ask them to leave most of what they really know, their wisdom and knowledge - their real mind power - at home when they go to school, college or work.

What's more, we don't teach them how to think. We don't educate them in the *true* sense of the word[2] about how they can learn, enjoy

---
2   From the Latin 'educere' meaning 'to draw out of'

learning, and continue learning constantly. We only want the narrow, limited skill set or capacity that applies to the equally limited course or job we have allotted to them, steeped in a fear that too much imagination, innovation, or, heaven forbid, fun at school or work might break the system we've carefully implemented to control the process.

Although we pay lip service to 'our people' being the most important factor in an organisation's success, how often is it really true? Frequently, people have become 'operationalized' and serve as cogs and levers in a machine that seeks to perpetuate itself, even though there is increasing proof that it isn't working. In the meantime, the spirit of humankind is diminished and along with it the spirit of the workplaces they inhabit, resulting in a malaise and lack of care that reflects in the true wealth, morale and spirit of the organisation, of the nation, of the planet.

Spirit at Work

Spirit permeates all organisations from the largest to the smallest; we can usually 'sense' the spirit of a place and its people almost immediately. There are big differences in how that spirit shows up. It's possible to walk into a place and be moved by the vitality and joy that's in the air. We simply know that the place is alive and well and that the people in it are resourceful and thriving.

Sometimes the spirit of a place seems trapped and limited, and it confines rather than freeing the people. So we might not find the spirit of that organisation pleasurable or sustaining, and if we work in such a place, it is unlikely we will be able to achieve our full potential.

Resourceful Spirit

As individuals we all have a resourceful spirit, but life can wear us down and dim the primal brilliance we all possess. The institutions we move through as part of the process of 'growing up' are not truly designed to nurture our spirits and let them soar, but to suppress and rein in our individuality, so we become malleable, educable (on the terms of the establishments offering said 'education') and ultimately 'employable'. Unleash too many free spirits and the system as it stands can't cope, so it's not in the interests of monolithic organisations to encourage flourishing, curious, energetic people who question the status quo. Even though the huge individual resources released in this way could, correctly husbanded, be the *exact* transformational breakthrough which is so needed.

Out of the Box

Through our lives we are put into boxes convenient to the system, and this leads to huge waste of potential. People (just like you) really **are** limitlessly creative, though you might not think so to look at the average town or corporation, or even at the typical government. It's becoming obvious that we can't sustain this waste of talent, that resources are being squandered, of which the most tragic is the waste of human resource. It's equally obvious that we need to urgently address the situation.

We're All Entrepreneurs Now

These days what we need is an entrepreneurial spirit that enlivens individuals and organisations alike. A pioneering, innovative approach that encourages people to be resourceful – to think independently, to regard themselves as a valuable asset, and thus foster the development of multiple skills and talents of all persuasions so that the individual is fulfilled, with the larger organisation, the nation, humanity and the planet ultimately served by creativity and innovation.

With the advent of 'The Big Society', cuts in funding, and the need for greater personal responsibility and resilience, it's time to take a stand and develop yourself to the best of your ability. Your ability, your true potential is likely to be far beyond that of which you currently dream – let us show you how to achieve more than you have thought possible, and become who you need to be to achieve all you want to achieve.

We live in a fiercely competitive world, where global choice is greater than ever before, and customers and clients have broader options and market intelligence readily (and instantly!) available through the Internet. Agility in spotting trends, organising and managing multiple ideas and strategies, and smart implementation are keys to success.

Several people I've interviewed recently for our magazine **ReSource** (including top US business coach **Marshall Goldsmith** and New York Times bestselling author and consultant **Marcus Buckingham**) have suggested that *'we're all entrepreneurs now'.* One unexpected current example in the UK is within the public sector, where funding cuts are changing the landscape dramatically. Situations are arising where employees, some of whom have been in their jobs for ten or fifteen years, are now obliged to re-apply for their existing posts - and are consequently required to 'sell' themselves again as the best possible candidate for the job. This requires the skill of knowing how to best position yourself, not something most public sector employees have previously had to consider. The ability to identify and promote your key assets, talents and expertise as benefits to your organisation thus becomes critical to successful job retention.

Transforming Business and Life

In this age of the changing world of work, when everyone, whether employed or running their own business, needs to adopt a more intelligently entrepreneurial mind-set, The Resourceful Mind helps fill a need for ways to develop clarity of thinking and effective methods to manage complexity and diversity, giving guidance and practical applications for being better in the business world - especially in the business of living productively and well.

Gifts, Talents and ....Failure?

There are many talented and gifted individuals whose abilities are undoubted, but they are not successful in terms of having a sustainable business which provides them with a good standard of living. They watch in frustration as others execute their ideas and projects and reap the rewards. They sometimes assume that success happens overnight and that they are unlucky or don't have the 'right' connections, so that's why they don't get the results they want so much. They are frustrated entrepreneurs, flitting from idea to idea, from seminar to seminar, buying into the latest technique or gizmo or software which they believe will transform their fortunes. But there are ways to transform this scenario.

Becoming a Resourceful Entrepreneur

Priming your mind for success and fulfilment

As a resourceful, successful entrepreneur, you know you need to be versatile, persistent and focused. You also need to be imaginative, quick witted and clear-thinking. You have to be able to orchestrate the mundane repetitive tasks that keep your show on the road - all the time keeping an eye on the bottom line - whilst retaining and developing your inspired vision for the future so you know where you are going, and what your purpose is. And you also need to stay open to new potential and shifts, keenly attuned to the rapid pace of change in our evolving world so you can adapt.

You have to manage relationships with staff, customers, suppliers, investors, partners, media and any other stakeholders in your organisation (and beyond), keep up to date with what's current in your sphere – and balance some time for personal relationships, family and leisure.

Inner and outer resources

"The Solution" has always been right where "you" are

You already have 'Inner Gold' within; often, that gold benefits from being drawn out, tempered and polished into a substance that withstands greater heat, pressure and buffeting, so you can thrive in challenging circumstances.

By developing your Resourceful Intelligence you prime the brain for learning – you turn on the part of the brain that forms the super highway to rapid adoption of more productive, sustainable behaviours that make you more successful. This is a great asset in your development as a successful business person and entrepreneur.

8 Key Criteria for Resourceful Entrepreneurs

Imagine you are interviewing yourself for your job as a very successful, fulfilled and happy entrepreneur: think of the resources – the qualities, skills, and talents - you need. Who do you need to be and become to fill that role? Do the attitudes, beliefs and values you hold support you?

Describe how you currently meet the criteria below:

1. **Business acumen** – e.g. understanding what today's 'experience economy' requires - Learn how to be in the most resourceful states so you prosper yourself and others by making better decisions. Getting to the heart of challenges, spotting new opportunities, accurately predicting beneficial trends and creating more success and wealth for yourself and others through advanced cooperative intelligence – RQ™

2. **Building & maintaining fruitful relationships, both business and personal** – e.g. rapport, caring, love, empathy, flexibility, collaboration, co-creation, understanding what other people want and need and how helping them achieve their goals brings benefits to all.

3. **Authenticity and Trust** – e.g. being real – dropping the masks - transparency, honesty, openness and adaptability are critical components for today's successful entrepreneurs and businesses – there are no secrets any more, you have to be your authentic self, walk your talk and embody the spirit of your organisation – what do you stand for? Who do you stand for?

4. **Persuading & Influencing with Impact and Integrity** – e.g. you need to be able to positively influence many people - family, children, friends, colleagues, clients, media - learn the psychology and key skills successful entrepreneurs use – understanding what makes people tick - what they never taught you in school about developing a powerful, magnetic presence based on mutual respect, compassion and genuine value

5. **Thinking** – e.g. taking personal responsibility for your thoughts - being resourceful, taking charge of and switching on the immense positive power of your mind – learning how your brain works, how it is 'plastic', how to change it for the better and how your thinking governs and can transform your life – allows you to stay a step ahead of the game - another thing they never taught you in school!

6. **Emotional resilience** – e.g. the ability to stay in balance, adapt, listen and respond appropriately even (or especially) when things get tough, making fair decisions despite adverse conditions

7. **Self-development** – e.g. understanding the positive difference it makes when you commit to transforming into who you need to become to achieve what you want to do, developing insight and self-awareness – offering the same opportunities for growth to your people - all organisations are made up of individual people who flourish and thrive through being nurtured and loved.

8. **Outstanding outcome orientation** – e.g. can balance long and short term needs and take account of consequences - doing well by doing good – recognising what is enough – fair and responsible values-based future visions - liking what you get versus getting what you think you'd like - the secret

chemical reaction that helps you easily stay focused on your projects – is keeping the end in mind so your compass is fixed unwaveringly on where you want to be the best way? – becoming holistic - understanding the importance of inclusion, and consideration of the present and future wellbeing of all – adopting a people, planet, prosperity approach.

Ask yourself:

- Who am I doing this for?
- What do I really, really want?
- What's the purpose?
- Where am I now?
- Where do I want to be?
- What prevents me?
- What else do I need?
- How will I achieve this?
- Who else can help me?
- What will happen if I do?
- What will happen if I don't?
- Is it okay to be successful?
- What does success mean to me?
- Who do I need to become to achieve what I want to achieve?

Being a resourceful entrepreneur

You know now that the resourceful entrepreneur is versatile, agile and fast – someone who can adjust to the constantly changing demands of a world which shifts not just from day to day, but often from moment to moment. This requires energy, persistence, and enthusiasm which are underpinned by inner strength and self-awareness, and ability to build and sustain relationships.

Resourceful Entrepreneur's Guide to Business in the 21st Century

A resourceful entrepreneur also requires imagination, analytical skills and action – ideas have to be **implemented** in order for anything to happen, otherwise our entrepreneur inhabits fantasy land and possesses an empire existing only on paper. Many highly creative entrepreneurs are abundant in their ideas, yet find it a challenge to actually get their projects to fly, or to maintain them in the longer term.

For you as an entrepreneur, this is where developing a Resourceful Mind is of key importance; it will assist you in fulfilling the criteria for being a successful entrepreneur, and also bring more balance and enjoyment into your life overall. After all, we start our businesses because we are passionate about our ideas, and because we want to liberate ourselves from the limits of a 'job'.

Once you've asked yourself these important questions, reflected on them, and noticed their implications, you will understand the importance of priming your mind for success and fulfilment. Re-connecting with what your business means to you and to the world, from a mind-set which allows you to be creative yet practical and put the full force of all your resources into action for success is a crucial step in becoming the truly resourceful person you have always secretly known you can be.

Christine Miller

To find out more about developing a Resourceful Mind
and becoming a Resourceful Entrepreneur see
www.resourcefulentrepreneur.com.

Ricardo Semler

President of Semco S/A, the Brazilian marine and food-processing machinery manufacturer, is internationally famous for creating the world's most unusual workplace.

Semler has been profiled in more than 200 magazines and newspapers, he was also profiled in Time's special edition, Time 100, which is published every 20 years to highlight global leaders. Named one of the Global Leaders of Tomorrow by the World Economic Forum in Switzerland, he has appeared on television and radio on four continents.

CIO magazine selected Semco as the only Latin American company among the most successfully re-engineered companies in the world. The BBC included Semco in its 'Re-engineering The Business', a series focusing on the world's five most successful management structures.

Semler was named Brazil's 'Business Leader of the Year' in both 1992 and 1990, the same year America Economia (The Wall Street Journals Spanish language magazine) named him Latin American Businessman of the Year. He is vice president of the Federation of Industries of Brazil and a board member of the SOS Atlantic Forest, Brazil's foremost environmental defence organisation.

Contact Ricardo Semler via:
Karen O'Donnell
t: + 353.1.230.2322
f: + 353.1.230.2306
e: KarenO@leighbureau.com
w: www.leighbureau.com

Chapter 2

Delegate Effectively

The Art and Science of Management by Omission

Ricardo Semler

By Christine Miller

> "I rarely attend meetings and almost never make decisions....
>
> We recently had a cocktail party to celebrate the ten-year anniversary since I last made a decision."

When Ricardo Semler took over his father's business, SEMCO, a Brazilian machinery manufacturer and service provider in 1982, he was 21 years old, and the company was almost bankrupt. After a short time following the conventional business model, Ricardo was stressed and under pressure – and he noticed that the entire organisation was also stressed and functioning inefficiently.

He decided that was a *'silly way to do business'*, and began to make radical changes. His innovative methods included getting rid of two-thirds of managers and eliminating all secretarial positions, allowing staff to choose their own working hours, and restructuring management resulting in a radically different organisation:

'SEMCO has no official structure. It has no organisational chart. There's no business plan or company strategy, no two-year or five-year plan, no goal or mission statement, no long-term budget. The company often does not have a fixed CEO. There are no vice presidents or chief officers for information technology or operations. There are no standards or practices. There's no human resources department. There are no career plans, no job descriptions or employee contracts. No-one approves reports or expense accounts. Supervision or monitoring of workers is rare indeed. There are no time clocks, dress codes, privileged office spaces or perks for top executives.'

Another of the many life-enhancing features of life at Semco is the Retire-a-Little-Programme. This allows employees to buy back their time to use for the things they love, whilst they are still in a position to truly enjoy them:

'So at SEMCO we introduced the, "retire-a-little programme". We say to you: Don't save your mountain-climbing for when you are 83. Your kids will be too old to take them to the movies in the afternoon when you are 83. Do it at 33. Buy your Wednesdays back from us and do what you would like to do when you retire. Then, after retirement, sell your Wednesdays to us again, so you will work with us one day a week and we don't lose all your expertise.'

With a turnover of over £100 million in 2005, SEMCO is now one of Brazil's fastest growing companies with an enviable staff retention level, high motivation and repeat customers who represent 80% of annual turnover.

Resource had a rare opportunity to talk to Ricardo Semler at the Leaders in London Summit, when we asked him about his current ideas and vision for the future.

TRANSFERABILITY

Christine: *Can you foresee your model, your methods being applied globally?*

Ricardo: We used to have a SEMCO tour. Thirty-five companies at a time would be given a tour and told how we do what we do. We had one tour every two weeks for years, and it was always over-subscribed. But not one of them took up what we do in full, because it entails giving up control. We have tracked sixteen organizations that ended up taking elements of what we do, but nobody wants to give up control totally and let everyone in the workforce lead.

There are a lot of essential anchor points or pillars which are similar over time, even though it is adapted. I'd say that to transfer the idea that working hours, the way work is defined, and the way careers are set up is silly is beginning to sound like common sense. There are more people now who understand that the idea of having a central headquarters and people moving across town to reach you, and having to design a career for themselves is largely ungratifying.

These days, it is easy for parts of our rationale to travel; companies could easily adapt it now, as more and more people are requesting this kind of flexibility. If people say, for example, *"how could I look at life and free time and retirement in a new way"*, companies could easily adapt to that. A lot of companies **will** adapt to that - not because they have read my book, but because times are changing and there are more people all the time requesting that kind of flexibility. One thing I was saying today, that has become more obvious to me, is that as you look at the people who actually flourish in the organisations that currently exist, you find that these are tough people. These are not reticent people - they are tough people who didn't mind elbowing others out of the way.

TALENT: TOUGH OR TENDER?

And the question is *'Can you really develop companies that are sustainable, and which are balanced over time, based on people who are tougher than everyone else?'* I think you cannot. So when you look at who this affects - it's true for women, it's true for shy people, for introverted people, it's true for very thoughtful people, intellectual people, all kinds of people who do not find their way up the corporate ladder, usually because they simply do not want to. This is something that is not very clear to organisations, they have the idea that the ones who made it up to the top are the ones who are very successful – that it is Darwinist, and these people got through the pack. But I think a lot of people actually actively choose not to do so; and if your organisation is willing to look for some of these, then you end up with a much better balance and a bigger pool of talent.

We recently ran an advertisement for a job opening which generated 3400 candidates. Now out of these 3400, there are probably 600 or 700 people who know that they would not be interested in the process anywhere else, in any other organisation. So perhaps we therefore have the pick of employees, a selection which is definitely not industry wide, and with this diversity we can generate something completely different.

There is the story of the hotel which we are building, where out of the 100 people we are employing, only 2 have any previous experience – none of the others have ever been in the hotel business before. We can't do anything with anybody who has been in the hotel business before – otherwise we are going to emulate other major hotel chains, and then rather than innovating, we will end up with a product that looks everybody else's.

Christine: *Tell me more about one of your other innovative projects, the school you are building – that piqued my interest; education can be an uninspiring experience.*

Ricardo: Education, as we usually see it, is preparing people for a very mediocre life. The process of giving away freedom, of becoming standardized, begins very young.

In our case we take kids from 2 – 14 years old, so what we say, which is very simple and comforting for the parents is – *we don't want kids in class who don't want to be in class, they have to want to come* – because we can't possibly teach a child something they are not interested in learning. If there is no interest, there is no retention. But it is also slightly scary for parents to think of that, of giving choice, even though it's only a 2 or 4 year old.

It is also scary for CEOs to imagine this scenario: in the business world what you are saying is '*can I trust people to come in to work at any time they want? These adults, can I trust them, can I know that they are going to spend all their time on the internet working just for me, and not sending emails to all their friends?*'. The question is: *can you possibly run an organisation if you* **don't** *trust people to do anything?* And the answer is - you cannot. Executives must give up control and trust the power of talent. Only then will that person's calling emerge.

TRUST

Christine: *Trust is a word, or a value, that you can easily take in to the working culture – if you go into a boardroom and start talking about love, for example, it's too soft and fluffy, but trust is acceptable.*

Ricardo: Trust is okay, because trust is deciphered in that corporate code as being something that someone else will do for *you* – the executive's thought is that '***they** will trust **me***'. But what we have to say to them is, '***you** have to trust **them**'* – and then the CEO says '*What do you mean? I want to know what time they come to work.*' It's not mutual trust – mutual trust is a much more complicated concept. But, '*they will have to trust that I am making the right decision*', that's something that executives can understand immediately.

And that's why they don't last – how long does an executive last these days, how long do companies last? Not very long, staff retention is very low. A key part of leadership is getting the right people. But recruitment today is like internet dating. Two dates and you get married forever? That's why turnover is so high.

So obviously this doesn't work – and therefore the idea that you are going to learn to do more of the same is not very exciting. In essence, if you think about it, it is like Freud's very simplistic solution which basically says that a composition of love and work is the only thing that matters.

Every time you throw one of these off-balance, the other one will never rebalance your life, so it's difficult to concentrate on just one or the other – to say *'Forget the people you love, forget your kids, just do the job right'* – and for what? More money? And then what do I do with that? Exchange it for a newer car, that's redder or greener than the one before?

In essence, humanity doesn't react well to this – they just do their nine-to-five thing, because they need what they get from that to go and do the things they really love.

If you can't make work into one of the things you really like, there is nothing left.

Christine Miller

Muhammad Yunus

The practical visionary who pioneered microcredit and, with his Grameen Bank, won the 2006 Nobel Peace Prize, has developed a new dimension for capitalism which he calls "social business." The social business model has been adopted by corporations, entrepreneurs, and social activists across the globe. Its goal is to create self-supporting, viable commercial enterprises that generate economic growth as they produce goods and services to fulfil human needs.

w: www.muhammadyunus.org
w: www.grameen-info.org

Chapter 3

Be Visionary

The 27 Dollar Miracle

Eradicating Poverty, Transforming Communities

Muhammad Yunus

by Christine Miller

A notable exemplar of the 21st century Zeitgeist Principle of 'doing well by doing good' is Nobel Peace prize winner Muhammad Yunus, Founder of Grameen Bank, the innovative 'microfinance' banking program. Yunus' book 'Creating a World without Poverty' impresses not only with its ideas, but more so with the fact that they are being practically applied with positive results in Bangladesh and beyond.

Individuals, families, and villages have been transformed and lifted out of poverty, not by charity hand-outs creating dependency, but by a programme of small microcredit loans which support people - mainly women - in setting up and running their own businesses within their communities. Conditions have been vastly improved for many, and families who could never have dreamt of giving their children an education have been enabled to do so; now their sons and daughters are returning to further benefit their communities with their medical and other professional expertise. In the past thirty years, microcredit has spread to every continent and benefited over

100 million families. This human capital investment based on trust is enriching the economic and social fabric and transforming lives beyond anything the conventional system ever believed possible or allowed.

The red tape and bureaucratic meanderings of that conventional system discourages individuals from making changes and challenging the status quo. Sometimes the problems of the world can seem far too great for one person's effort to make any difference, so we devolve the responsibility for change back to our governments, to organisations – or to just about anywhere else but at our own doorstep.

But Yunus' story about what prompted him to take action against poverty in Bangladesh back in 1976 is a prime example of the *real* effects that one person's persistent, thoughtful approach can make to a whole region. In this case, the region is one of the poorest and most fragile ecological systems in the world, a place prone to ever-increasing cyclones and flooding, where the effects of global warming are acutely felt - a place where, in 1974, a famine led to the deaths of millions of people.

DRIVE TO ERADICATE POVERTY

Muhammad Yunus tells us how his continuing quest to eradicate poverty began.

We had a terrible famine in the country if you recollect in 1974. Many people died: not from disease or epidemic, but from simply not having enough to eat for survival. People died; not hundreds of them, not thousands of them, not hundreds of thousands of them, but *millions*. So that's our journey; and when you live in Bangladesh you go through frustration after frustration. Nothing seems to work; but you don't give up hope. You continue to fight back. In an environment of such frustrations, many people in Bangladesh tried to do many different things to overcome the frustration and bring out rays of hope.

POWER OF ONE PERSON'S EFFORTS

When you see the famine raging everywhere, you become totally numb, not knowing what you can do in a situation like that. I was a teacher at one of the universities in Bangladesh, and I was hoping that, as a human being, I could still do something. I felt I shouldn't be overwhelmed by the vastness of the problem.

All I was trying to do in the village next to the university campus was to see if I could do something for just *one person*, even for a day. I was not trying to change everything in the next village; I thought if I can help one person at a time, even if it was only for one day, then that will be good enough for me. This was the process that I got involved with, and I felt more at ease than just sitting around and watching what was happening in front of me, and not knowing what to do.

THE 27 DOLLAR MIRACLE

Then I began to find out what terrible things went on inside the village. There was 'loan-sharking', lending tiny amounts of money to people, and controlling their lives because of the debt. I thought I should understand this a little better, and find out how it happens. After several days of going around the village I made a list of people who were borrowing from the money lenders. When the list was complete, there were 42 names on that list and the total money they borrowed was just $27. I was shocked that people had to suffer so much for such a small amount of money. At the same time it dawned on me, the problem is very intricate but the solution is so simple.

The idea came to my mind that if I give this $27 to all these 42 people according to the list I have, and ask them to return the money to the loan-sharks then they will be free. So I immediately did that. But I didn't realise what it would lead to next!

What surprised me was the enormous amount of excitement that it generated in these families. They looked at it as if I had done something that was a miracle. In the beginning I just felt amused; amused by the $27 miracle. I said that with just $27 you can become an angel - if you can spare another $27 you may become a super angel! So the thought that came to my mind was *'if you can make so many people so happy with such a small amount of money, then why shouldn't you do more of it?'* That's exactly what I wanted to do.

CHALLENGING CONVENTION

I thought about the ways I could do that, and one idea caught my imagination. I thought I should ask a bank located in the campus to lend the money to the people in the village, just a few yards away from each other. When I went to the bank manager and suggested this, he said, *'absolutely no way. The bank cannot lend money to the poor people'.*

That is the biggest lesson I learned about banking. I had no idea how banking was done, but he repeatedly explained that it is impossible for a bank to do that. The more I insisted, the more he put up resistance. So it went on for several months, talking to the senior officials in the banking hierarchy. Nobody would accept that idea.

Finally, I used some of their rules to make it easy for them to understand. I said, *'why don't you accept me as a guarantor, I'll sign all your papers. I'll take your risk. You keep your rule and I get the money'.* So it took another couple of months to push them. Finally, they accepted me as a guarantor and then I took the money and gave it to people. I wanted to make sure people found it easy to pay the money back. So I came up with tiny little ideas to make it easy for them, and it worked.

That was the beginning of Grameen Bank - with $27, and then it grew and grew.

TURNING BANKING ON ITS HEAD

So what did we really do that made it happen? In a way, we can look at it as if we are mimicking the conventional banks in a very strange way. As if whenever you needed a rule to see how to handle it, we looked at the conventional banks and how they do it. Once we find out how they do it, we just do the opposite! And it works, and it works beautifully, and it's still working.

Conventional banks are based on the principle, the more you have, the more you get. We reversed that principle. We said the less you have - the higher attention you get. If you have absolutely nothing, you get the highest loan. Conventional banks want collateral, you have to bring wealth and position, before you get a loan. We reversed it, we said forget about collateral. In our system there is no collateral, there is no guarantee. In our system there are no lawyers; in conventional banks anything you do, they will bring a lawyer, all the papers you have to sign, seal, and notarise. We don't have any system. Conventional banks go to men to give the money, we go to women. They go to the rich, we go to the poor.

They want you to know everything about your business; when they are convinced, only then they will talk business. We go to women, and they say *'well I don't know many things'.* The more she insists, the more she says *'I don't know anything, I never touched money in my life'*, the more we get interested in them. So you can see in every way, it is the opposite, and it has been working very well.

TRANSFORMING COMMUNITIES

Today Grameen Bank has seven and a half million borrowers, and 97% are women. The Bank is owned by them, and it has changed their lives. Not only does it work in Bangladesh, it now works all over the world, in rich countries and poor countries; countries in Latin America; countries in Africa; countries in Asia. You look around and you see that with their ability, their creativity, people are changing their economic situation. They are moving out of poverty. They are sending their children to school. Grameen Bank gives loans for sending children to higher education, so that illiterate families can have children who are literate and educated and going into higher education. Right now we have over 21,000 students in Grameen Bank who are in medical schools, engineering schools, and universities, and some of them have scholarships from international institutions such as Harvard.

When I go to the villages and meet these women who have been working so hard to make a difference to their life, it's an amazing experience to be with them. Now I see a new phenomenon coming, added to that. When I'm visiting them, the daughter from the city comes in: she's just finished her degree, she's a Doctor now, and she's practising as an internee at the hospital. She came because I was visiting her village. So I see the mother and the daughter standing side by side. One is a totally illiterate person who joined Grameen Bank some 10 or 15 years back, took tiny loans $50, $20 or whatever, started her life and sent her daughter to school. Now, she is a doctor.

RELEASING HUMAN POTENTIAL

You cannot escape the thought in your mind, looking at these two ladies standing next to each other, that her mother could have been a doctor, too. But society never gave her mother a chance. All we have done through Grameen Bank is allow her to improve her income, given her the capacity to send her daughter to school and encouraged her to keep the child in school. Then we gave her a student loan to continue and finish her education, and she became a doctor. Her mother must have the same elements in her; there is no reason why she should have any less than her daughter has.

Then you will also have the mother who will be introducing her own mother; the older lady stays inside the house because she's not used to being in a crowd. So she's still a shy old woman, whose daughter has been to Grameen Bank, and has changed her life in a different way. The grandmother has never been through such an experience, but when you meet her, again that same question comes to your mind - she could have been a doctor, too.

The conclusion that you would come to is that poverty is not in the person; poverty is not created by the person, poverty is created by the system. Therefore if you want to address the issue of poverty, it's not about her, it's about us. What did we do wrong? Where *did* we go wrong? Fix it up. If we can pick out the seeds of poverty that we have put inside all the things that we build as institutions - the policies, the concepts, then nobody in the world would be a poor person. There's nothing, absolutely nothing wrong in the human being. We messed it up, and then blamed them.

THE END OF POVERTY

At the end of Muhammad Yunus' book, he suggests that when we have eradicated poverty, then we should create 'Poverty Museums'; *'When there are no poor people anywhere in the world, then in the same way that there are no longer any dinosaurs in the world, and just as we keep the skeletons of dinosaurs in museums and we take our children to see what the dinosaurs used to be like, so we will take our children to the poverty museum to show what poverty used to be like'.*

We have here a model that works, that *is* working, transforming some of the most deprived communities in the world. Today, all we need to do is fix the date: which is the year in which we will set up that Poverty Museum?

Christine Miller

Robbie Steinhouse

Robbie is an ICF certified coach and an NLP University certified NLP Trainer. He is also an entrepreneur. In 1987 he started Gray's Inn Estates, and in 1998 Residents Insurance Services Limited: these businesses insure and manage over 60,000 properties. In 2002 he changed focus and started the Coaching Consultancy and NLP School Europe. The former arranges business coaching, while the latter runs public courses in NLP, from one-day seminars on NLP in business to full Practitioner training. Married with two daughters, he lives in Highgate, London, U.K.

t: +44(0)20 7 428 7915
e: info@nlpschool.com
w: www.nlpschool.com

Chapter 4

Think Strategically

Think Like an Entrepreneur

Robbie Steinhouse

We normally associate the word 'entrepreneur' with Richard Branson, Anita Roddick or the panel on Dragons' Den – highly successful people who have built enormous businesses. However there are other levels of entrepreneurship. A 'lifestyle' entrepreneur is someone who runs their own business for themselves, maybe with one or two other people. Does that sound like you? Congratulations, you are an entrepreneur, too.

Lifestyle entrepreneurs do not have to be as dynamic or charismatic as the builders of great businesses, but if you can emulate some ways in which great entrepreneurs think, you will find running your own small business much easier.

In this piece, I want to look at one aspect of the entrepreneurial mind-set, and present an NLP-based model to integrate it into your life.

Entrepreneurs have to master all the skills needed to run a business. In a large business, no one person has all these: there are specialist marketers, sales people, accountants, purchasers, technologists (etc.) In a lifestyle business, one person has to have them all: you.

There are numerous ways of classifying these skills. I break them down into four groups, and call them 'Capability Sets' as a reminder that in terms of NLP Logical Levels, they are capabilities (i.e. skills), not beliefs or values, so they can be learnt quite easily.

Almost all new entrepreneurs are good at one or two of these, adequate at another but can be appalling at another. Wise ones make it their business to plug this 'hole' as quickly as possible, by reading, by finding an expert and firing questions at them, by attending formal courses of study and, of course, by learning from experience. Other aspiring entrepreneurs take a different route, ignoring the holes, thinking 'they don't really matter' or 'It'll be fine'. Then they wonder why their businesses fail.

Capability Set 1 - Leadership.

This set covers those overall skills that you need as a business leader – for that is what you are, even if, for the moment, the business is just you. These skills include the ability to *motivate and manage people* – especially the ability to motivate and manage yourself: entrepreneurs are self-starters and get things done. The ability to *innovate* is another key skill: not so much great technical innovation as mental agility and the ability to improvise. Leaders need to understand and to formulate *strategy*, a vision of where you are headed, and, behind that, a vision of how you will get there. What are you in business for? How is what you do going to help other people (who, in turn, will pay for the help they receive)? How will you deliver that help to them? How will you let them know about the help you offer?

Capability Set 2 - Administration and Operations.

Books on entrepreneurship tend to emphasize the first capability set above. Leadership is romantic, exciting stuff. But much of entrepreneurial success comes from capability set 2: the apparently dull business of just 'getting stuff done'. This set of inward-looking, practical skills.

Administration is the basic running of your business – getting tax returns in on time, answering emails (etc.).

Operations is about doing what you have to do to deliver your product or service repeatedly, reliably and profitably.

Though it sounds dull, good entrepreneurs often enjoy this part of the business.

Capability Set 3 - Finance and Legal.

These are essentially protective capabilities.

Many small businesses suffer from poor financial skills – lack of cash is the most common cause of business failure. This is an area where many lifestyle entrepreneurs feel they are weak.

This weakness must be addressed. Confront any fears you may have of maths or figures; read a book like *Finance on a Beermat* by Stephen King, Jeff Macklin and Chris West; learn the basic 'money-watching' techniques such as double-entry bookkeeping, simple profit and loss accounts, balance sheets and cash-flow management. They aren't that difficult.

**Capability Set 4 - Sales, Marketing and generally
    'making friends for the business'.**

This is the capability set that looks at, and relates to, the world out there.

Sales is often seen as work for smooth-talking charmers, and such people do often end up in sales. But note two things.

> **One:** a lot of sales is about process – getting lists of prospects, 'qualifying' them (finding out which people on the list are actually worth pursuing), setting up sales visits, following up. These are capabilities, which can be learnt.

> **Two:** every business person has to do sales, whether they like it or not. If you have a belief that you can't do sales, change it!

Marketing is often seen as something only big businesses do, but this is not the case. Every business person has to learn about the people they are selling to – what they really want, how they like to buy, how they make decisions – and then present what they do or make in the light of that.

A business needs customers above all, but also other, more general *friends of the business,* a wider circle of relationships with people such as mentors, suppliers, 'evangelists' (those nice people who go round telling others what a good service you have provided). NLP can be particularly helpful in winning and keeping such friends. Cultivate rapport; try and experience their model of the world.

So there we have the four key sets of capabilities for running a business:

- **Leadership:** holding it all together and making sure it goes in the right direction.

- **Operations:** actually doing whatever it is you do.

- **Finance/Legal:** keeping it safe and healthy.

- **Sales** and other outward-facing skills.

And you need to become good at them all.

Some writers on entrepreneurship say that you should get other people to fill in the 'holes', where your skills are weak. I do not think this is right. Up to a point, of course, you can do this. By all means have an accountant do your tax return rather than become an expert on the Byzantine intricacies of the tax system. But don't treat this person as an excuse for not mastering the financial basics of your business.

There are two main reasons for this. Neither is the paranoid 'you can't trust anybody', by the way!

The first is that if you do 'outsource', you still have to manage the outsourced person. They may provide advice as well as a service, but in the end *you* have to decide based on their advice, and unless you understand that advice, you will be unable to choose whether to act on it or not.

The second is that to make good decisions, you need to be able to see your business from the four perspectives outlined above. If, for example, you have no concept of what is safe or what is unsafe, you will make rash decisions. I have developed a technique for anchoring the necessary perspectives and accessing them rapidly to ensure that you look at an issue from all the relevant perspectives.

This enables you to anchor four states that relate to each of the above **capability sets.**

The first state you need to access is that of an Innovator (part of the first, or leadership capability set). Think of a time when anything seemed possible and you were being creative. Enjoy this feeling of possibility, imagination, creativity... When you have a strong sense of being imaginative and creative, anchor that state onto the knuckle of your *index* finger.

Next, anchor the 'operations' capability, the Doer. Think of a time when you were either getting on with something, or making a clear, rigorous plan of how you were going to get on with something. Enjoy the buzz of activity. When you have a strong sense of this, anchor the state onto the knuckle of your *middle* finger.

Next, anchor the 'protective' role of an External Advisor such as an accountant or lawyer. I find it best to see this person as both critical and caring. Their role is to look at options and consider what might go wrong. (Note that they are not just criticizing for the hell of it!) Think of a time when you realized things were suddenly getting out of control and you seized back that control, stopping activity and subjecting your current position to rigorous analysis. When you have a strong sense of being analytical, aware of danger and in control, anchor this to the knuckle of your *ring* finger.

Finally anchor the perspective that focuses on the world out there, the world of Stakeholders in the company – customers, markets, the public in general. The state you want to access here is one of empathy. Think of a time when you were really attuned to someone else; you knew how they thought and felt, without knowing how you knew this (and they let you know that you were right – this wasn't just mind-reading plus wishful thinking). When you have a strong sense of this, anchor this state to the knuckle of your *little* finger.

Now bring to mind the project you are thinking about.

Fire the Innovator anchor and brainstorm lots of ideas. Be very optimistic and create an ideal scenario for a year or two's time.

Fire the Doer anchor and put together a practical plan to get to that scenario. Be specific – what's the first step, the second, the third? The Doer is also a planner, and very good at this kind of meticulous work.

Fire the External Advisor anchor and ask yourself: what could go wrong? You should end up with a set of criticisms of the plan.

Fire the Stakeholder anchor and consider how the action will impact on other people such as a typical customer, a key supplier or a family member.

Return to the Innovator and come up with solutions to the issues raised by the External Advisors. Balance the needs of people 'out there' who are resistant to the plan and those who want to be involved.

Spend time not touching any knuckle; this is when you are using another part of the Leadership Capability, that of the decision maker.

Repeat as necessary.

This process can be used with any decision. Don't overuse it, though, by applying it to every decision you make. Some decisions are too small; just decide and do.

As a final thought about 'thinking like an entrepreneur', I would stress the old motto 'don't sweat the small stuff'. Running our own businesses we face small decisions every day. Agonize about them, and we will get bogged down. Decide then act! But if a big decision comes along, take time, use the IDEAS model and bring all the four capability sets to bear on it.

That way you will decide well.

Robbie Steinhouse

Lord Andrew Mawson

Andrew Mawson is one of the UK's leading social entrepreneurs. Over 25 years he has created a family of projects in particular the renowned Bromley-by-Bow Centre in East London. Today he is leader, motivator and adviser to major projects including the St. Paul's Way Transformational project in the London Borough of Tower Hamlets and Water City, a visionary plan to revitalise East London and a vehicle for Olympic legacy.

www.amawsonpartnerships.com

Book:

The Social Entrepreneur

Making Communities Work

Andrew Mawson

Published by: Atlantic Books

2008

£9.99

w: www.groveatlantic.co.uk

ISBN 978-1-843546-61-0

Chapter 5

Learn by Doing

Getting Real: Leaving a Lasting Legacy

Lord Andrew Mawson

There is currently much debate about legacy, about building sustainable communities, about involving 'hard to reach' groups, and empowering those on the fringes of society to take charge of their own lives. There are countless policy papers and politicians, committees and consultants putting forward ideas – a lot of talk, but how much action? Who and where are the people who are *really* making a difference and implementing projects that work, with demonstrable results over a period of time? And is the funding used for development and redevelopment *really* reaching out to those who need it?

Social Entrepreneurship

One way in which projects are being effectively implemented at grass roots level is through 'Social Entrepreneurship'. This is a current buzz phrase, a growing trend, with social entrepreneurs emerging as a distinctive band of potential change-makers with a unique role to play in developing a self-sustaining, independent and responsible society.

"Social entrepreneurs are to be found in all sectors of our society – in business, in the voluntary sector, in the public sector; on the high street and in the boardroom and in ordinary living rooms up and down

the country. They are difficult to define precisely because they are being entrepreneurial – and the moment you define and categorize entrepreneurship, it will shift shape and render your definition obsolete. If it works, it works, no matter how you're defining it."
P. 164 'The Social Entrepreneur'

Although the term may be relatively new, the ideas behind it are not. Britain has a long history and tradition of such ventures, including co-operative societies and the pioneering work done by families such as father and son Joseph and Seebohm Rowntree in the 19th century.

Real People, Real Projects

Movements are now springing up around the world, proposing and embracing numerous admirable and worthy projects to alleviate poverty, exclusion and suffering for those whose social, economic and geographical conditions are challenging. I have been exploring the topic, and I was looking for live examples of real people working on the ground with successful projects, those who were overcoming practical difficulties and thriving, rather than movements or groups with ideas but little action.

Lord Andrew Mawson OBE is one of Britain's original, real, hands-on social entrepreneurs. I discovered him through his superbly engaging book, *"The Social Entrepreneur"*, (Atlantic Books 2008) which I devoured in one sitting. With over two decades of practical experience in building grass roots communities that really *do* meet the needs of their members, and are sustainable because they are shaped by the active participation and guidance of those who live in and use them, he fitted my profile perfectly.

Bromley-by-Bow – a model community

Based on 'learning by doing' rather than on policy papers and academic theory, and firmly embracing human creativity and diversity, the Bromley-by-Bow Centre, established by Andrew Mawson in 1984 is located *"in one of the most historically socially 'failing' parts of the country"*, and serves as a real focal point for the community. The Centre provides healthcare and education, creates jobs, and generates wealth for the area, delivering services in new ways to overcome the daily difficulties in people's lives. As you will discover when you read the book, it was not an easy journey, and there were many difficulties to overcome and lessons to learn. Bureaucracy, red tape, failure to listen (and act) by official bodies, and developing the patient perseverance required to work out how best to collaborate across a diverse range of backgrounds, needs and cultures, to name a few.

His efforts have been publicly recognised, and he was awarded a Life peerage in 2007, but Andrew Mawson is keen to point out that he is a 'cross-bencher'. In other words, an independent not attached to any political party. His role in the House of Lords is to offer his expertise and practical know-how wherever it is most needed. By leading debates, holding symposiums and guiding his peers on live tours, he is again taking the initiative, introducing them to a world where *real* results have been achieved for *real* people by listening to, involving and honouring local communities.

Regeneration and the 2012 Olympic Legacy

The London 2012 Olympics is an area of considerable interest and importance to Lord Mawson, not least because his 'patch' of East London in Bromley-by-Bow sits right on the doorstep of the Olympic redevelopment site. As Mawson says:

'I have lived and worked in the Lower Lea Valley in the East End of London for nearly 25 years. In 1984, I founded the Bromley by Bow Centre, which is 300 yards from the Olympic site. I have worked with a team of very able people and members of the local community to grow a community project which has gained a national and international reputation in community development and innovative approaches to the delivery of health, education and other public services.'

He is determined that the regeneration and attendant vast investment (some £9.5 billion) should provide a lasting, long term and living legacy to the local community, rather than producing a wasteland abandoned after the event, as has happened in other countries. His major concern is that the opportunity for **real** legacy may be missed in the bureaucratic and administrative process which often ignores **real** needs. Just as we went to print, London Mayor Boris Johnson added his voice to the pressing concern that current legacy policy is in danger of missing the mark and consequently failing to deliver lasting benefits to the East London communities who need it most.

I met with Lord Mawson at the House of Lords...... What is your current biggest project and what is the inspiration driving it?

One of the biggest projects I'm involved in is **'Water City'**, a large regeneration scheme in the East End of London. 'Water City' is, in essence, the long term legacy of the Olympics.

Tell me more about the issues of Olympic legacy.

On January 17th 2008 I led a debate in the House of Lords, on the subject of what *is* the real Olympic legacy. My concern is that the true legacy is in danger of being missed, through lack of collaboration and attention to detail. Social entrepreneurs are now partnering with business to develop pieces of the city, which is really challenging the traditional way of doing regeneration.

We are trying to help the people who are responsible for putting the Olympics together to understand the history of East London. For example, East London has been driven by water for 250 years; around us in Bromley-by-Bow there are five and a half miles of waterways, and the Docklands drove the British economy for a long time. If you get to know the residents of East London - and the social entrepreneurs *must* know the people - then you know that all their families and lives are connected to water.

Many of our population are from Bangladesh, and Bangladesh is profoundly connected to water. Those of us who work with families in the area know how water, the old docks and their histories are inextricably linked together. If you want a legacy that has integrity and reality about it, then build on the history of the place; don't reinvent it, and don't land from Mars and think, *'well, we've got this bright idea'*. Build on what is there.

So this is a vision for East London's future?

Yes, it is. 'Water City' is saying: *'This is the vision of the future of East London, developed by people who live and work there who have been involved for years; and underneath this vision, rests a whole social entrepreneurial culture that's been cooking for 25 years, and, by the way, is developing now with big business'.*

Key business partners like Arup (a leading design firm) are seeing this, and if we can break through the glass ceiling, then it has a potential, over the next period of time, to really flower. The Olympics is a fantastic catalyst, but it will come and go. It's a great catalyst, but it's more than a park, it's more than just an Olympic case.

This is about building a new Metropolitan district of London, with business entrepreneurs and social entrepreneurs, and demonstrating in practice what legacy means for real people and their children. Not *'here's a theory about legacy'* which is very woolly, with a few pictures of politicians turning up, smiling, having their photos taken. That's not 'Legacy'.

It is intensely practical, and there is a real opportunity for Olympic legacy to build on what works, what we know and have demonstrated works. We need the barriers down. There's a big 11-mile blue fence around the Olympic site at the moment; if you really want legacy - *don't hide behind the fence!* What we need to do is to start winding the strands of gold from the outside of the fence onto the inside of the fence, and if we do it slowly, then over a few years you might find that the legacy emerges in a far more real way. The 'Water City' proposals are what we are developing with business; this is really the long term, 20-year legacy of the Olympics, this £20 billion of investments for the next twenty years.

Does this have implications beyond London and the UK?

We could really lift the game here, begin to show exactly how you do real legacy, and demonstrate how you could justify a £9.5 billion pound spend in countries in Africa or India. But if we just carry on doing regeneration, as Governments have always done it, and the IOC have always done it - nothing will be changed in the longer term.

Spending £9 billion in the area will of course make a difference - don't get me wrong, we welcome the investment—but the key questions are:

- **Are we investing the money well?**
- **Will it make a sustainable difference?**
- **Will it deliver the maximum added value to local communities?**
- **Will it transform East London for the next 100 years?**
- **Or will a great opportunity have been lost?**

The Devil in the Detail – one of your favourite phrases?

Lord Peyton of Yeovil, who was a patron of the Bromley-by-Bow Centre for 17 years, said this:

"government understands the shape of the forest but has no idea what is actually going on under the trees".

Those words of wisdom accurately described my experience over many years in East London as I watched endless regeneration schemes, NHS structures and the like come past our doors. When you stay in one place for a very long time you watch successive government programmes. Their effect on people's lives is often quite different from the intention of the rhetoric that launched them.

Social entrepreneurs and business are beginning to show new ways of doing real legacy, but the old systems and most of the IOC and government are still out of date. We're trying to break through a gap in a glass ceiling, and say *'sorry, the devil in the detail of what's happening in East London may have some real international implications; but it's not going to happen unless there's real leadership out there that understands the devil in the detail of what we're doing'*.

We are building on 25 years of work; it's not a policy paper. It requires real, courageous political leadership to allow a new thing to break through the glass ceiling. Our belief is that legacy is not just about land and buildings, as I fear much of the present Olympic rhetoric suggests, but about people, places and sustainable communities.

What are your thoughts on Social Entrepreneurship and its relationship to ending poverty?

The way out of poverty; well, we have found that the way into these big questions is to always start with small things, with the micro. What we've found is that simply giving people grants or handouts in East London sometimes creates real dependencies, which has similarities with the Third World. It's not the solution. What one has to do is create circumstances where people really begin to participate and take responsibility for projects in the environment – such as a 3 acre park, as in the example in the book, and come together to build a new heath centre, and new housing.

Releasing Potential

What happens with local residents when you involve them in projects is that you suddenly release potential. One East End mother now chairs a £300 million property company. Of course, she didn't do it from day one, but she's learned that she has real skills. At a board meeting she can confidently face up to lawyers, because she *is* very bright, she's not stupid. You find that people are beginning to take responsibility for some of these things in real ways. And that's real empowerment; that's moving away from *'give me a handout'*, to *'give me a hand up'*. We've had a lot of experience with real people with names and addresses doing that. In East London it's growing to another scale now and that's the great opportunity. I visited some big companies in Australia, where endless politicians and policymakers were showing me graphs, but no one ever mentioned anyone with a name and address. I think social entrepreneurs worth their salt are interested in people's names and addresses, and ask, *'What actually happened to this person?'* That's the real test. Don't give me statistics, don't give me meaningless policies - *show me real individuals from real places.*

What special message do you have for readers?

I think the point is that there *is* a new world emerging here. In the book, I describe how people worry about all the complicated problems we face in the world. Some get quite depressed, feeling there is nothing they can do.

They look at these big issues and wonder:

'How on earth can little old me affect this?'

My message is that the way into these big, big issues is through the micro, as any business person knows. First, understand in detail how one store works, before building a national chain of 2000.

Social entrepreneurs are beginning to pioneer new ways of doing things, and that's fantastic. This is where the opportunity lies; we need more of the right businesses to get into bed with us, so that we can grow.

It requires innovation, and that requires *'learning by doing cultures'*, moving beyond policy papers and talking cultures.

That's how we'll refresh our constitution and our democracy, and make it real for people. The clues are there in the micro, they're appearing, but not enough attention is being paid to the detail. Life is full of messy details; people don't fit into policy papers, and real life is complicated. Often, social entrepreneurs are not smooth people, they're not civil servants, and they *are* real. They get hold of the issue, and that's what we need; some of these things are very uncomfortable, but that's life. It might be about backing the people who seem difficult, because they are tackling issues in a real way.

There are a lot of people out there who have been classified as a 'problem'. As we have found in East London – *the fact is, they are not a problem, they're just bored. They want to use their energy rather more honestly and creatively. That's what we have to address.*

There is much more to do…. and a lot further to go.

Christine Miller

Nicola Cairncross

Nicola works with bright, professional people who are always seeking to enhance their financial intelligence. Learn how to make your money last longer than your month, profit from your passion, or develop passive income flows via The Financial Intelligence Programme. She has been featured in the Times on Saturday, the Financial Mail on Sunday, the Observer Money and Red Magazine.

e: nicola@nicolacairncross.com
w: www.nicolacairncross.com

Paperback: 228 pages
Publisher: Lean Marketing Press
Language English
ISBN 13: 978-0-954568-18-4

Chapter 6

Market Organically

Natural Marketing for Lone Rangers

Nicola Cairncross

"Ooooooh," you may say, "I could NEVER be good at marketing, I'm just not that sort of person. I'm not pushy enough".

Well, if that is your reaction to the title of this article, I would like to kick off by giving you permission to hate marketing (and its cousin, "sales").

I am not going to try to turn you into a marketeer or a salesperson - but will you open your mind (just a chink!) to the possibility that you CAN stay just as you are and STILL be more successful at what you do?

Marketing and sales are inextricably linked in most people's mind and everyone knows sales people are scuzz-bags - right? The very words "marketing" and "sales" conjures up images of people being brainwashed by ads and parted from their money, in exchange for something they don't want. By men in dodgy suits!

Well, the first concept to get your head around is that people are generally very sophisticated and astute. You cannot sell people something they don't want, no matter how heavy handed your tactics. And generally, even by very clever marketing, you cannot persuade or brainwash people into wanting something, that they hadn't wanted before.

Secrets Revealed

How would it be if we started thinking of marketing as the art of letting people know about a product or service that they already want, but didn't know where to go or which one to choose. How would it be if we made our service so good, so excellent, that if WE were introduced to it, we would be DELIGHTED to be told about that service. How about thinking of marketing as simply making sure that our excellent service is not being kept a secret?

What about the sales part of the process? The dreaded "closing" that everyone seems to find so hard. What is a "close", anyway? It's actually just asking someone if - having been recommended, having voiced their needs, knowing your fees, reassured that you can help - you ask them if they would like to book an appointment. Offering an appointment on a Tuesday or a Thursday is an "alternative close". Technical stuff, eh?

So marketing is about not being a secret, and selling is about making an appointment. Easy - we can do that! But what if we could make it even easier? Have I got your interest?

How do we go about not being a secret? The traditional ways to market anything are by creating a brochure, business cards and letterhead, advertising, mailing out to prospective purchasers (or clients) and selling your services to them. An expensive and time consuming business. Does your heart sink when you read this? Well, I have some good news. None of that works - or only 2% of the time anyway! So what does work?

Create a Reservoir

What you need to do is simply create a reservoir of people who know about you, who like what you do, and who ONE DAY might use your services. Oh boy! When my first business coach, told me this, I breathed a big wonderful sigh of relief.

How big should your reservoir be? Popular wisdom says that it should be in excess of 1000 to generate an almost effortless work flow, but that you start to attract clients at about 400-500 people if you are in a specific niche market.

How do you fill your reservoir and with whom? This is where you start to think about your ideal client - because who wants a reservoir of less than ideal clients? The first people on your list should be your existing clients - or at least those you want to keep. You see, this is one of the big secrets about marketing, it's as much about weeding out the clients you don't want, as attracting the clients you do want! Think about the qualities of your ideal client, what are they like (TIP: think about your existing clients and pick out the A-List). I'll share the qualities of my ideal client to give you an idea.

The Ideal Client

My ideal coaching client is bright, articulate, educated (by life, if not uni!) fast on the uptake, action orientated, entrepreneurial (or would like to be), definitely has email, is successful by anyone else's standards but perhaps not achieving their potential yet. They may feel overwhelmed and take on too much. They probably talk too fast and walk as if they are in a hurry. They are serious about wanting to improve their business or their life and they are prepared to set aside some time to come to calls and to take some action. They don't cancel or re-arrange calls, they pay on time and they appreciate my coaching. They are not ashamed to say they have a coach and they recommend me to everyone they meet!

Grade your existing clients into, **A** clients (love you, come regularly, pay happily, turn up, recommend you all the time), **B** clients (love you, come fairly regularly, pay happily, turn up, sometimes recommend you), **C** Clients (think you are ok, come occasionally, pay happily, turn up, never recommend you) and the **D** Clients (aka the BMW's - bitchers, moaners and whiners). What do we do right now with the D Clients? D is for Dump. Dumping the D's makes more time to give the A's and the B's more time, more service, more attention.

So how do we meet more A Clients and get them in our reservoir? Work out who the A's are and where they hang out. Are they business people? Mums At Home or Ladies Who Lunch? Sports players?

When you have established who they are, then think about the problems they have and the things they are interested in. Think about ways you could add value to those A List Clients. It might be sending out clippings from newspapers on articles of interest, it might be creating a simple A4 two sided newsletter, it might be a website with useful links and an email newsletter, it might be writing for specialist publications (the last two being my preferred methods, hence this article!). Just put yourself in their shoes for a moment.

Enjoy Yourself

But whichever method you choose, make sure you enjoy it. Say what? Yes, you have my permission to only choose marketing methods that you actually enjoy. Why? Because if you don't enjoy them, you won't do them - even if your business is falling down around your ears.

I remember Fiona, my Reiki Master and therapist client. She found that she was massaging a client or two in the morning, then nothing at all till the evening, when her working clients turned up. She wanted to build up her lunchtime and afternoon clientele and then limit her evenings to two per week. Who would be able to come at those times? The ladies who lunch and the self-employed. Where do the ladies hang out? At charity events and hairdressers and in nice restaurants. What are their challenges? To look after themselves to the n'th degree, be well groomed, relaxed and charming at all times. She joined her local ladies groups, talked to her hairdresser and beauty therapist about a joint marketing initiative, volunteered for the local large charity committee and attended a few lunches herself, and then, to reach the self-employed business person, joined her local business breakfast club, BNI (Business Networking International - for details see www.bni.com).

The self employed do not have enough time to look after themselves and often suffer from stress and bad backs. Fiona initially started talking about bad backs and sports injuries, and now her business has taken off in an amazing way. People went for their practical problems initially but now go for the Reiki and the other types of emotional healing. She was so nervous talking about her service for 60 seconds at first, but now is completely at home in that environment. She even demonstrated crystal therapy the other morning and it was a real treat to watch hard bitten businessmen handling rose quartz and feeling the warmth coming off the crystals.

Finding What Suits You

This route is not for everyone, but one thing is for sure, there is a marketing method that will suit you. I like meeting people and writing, so I have a website, a monthly financial coaching newsletter, I write articles for magazines and I attend every networking lunch, breakfast and dinner that I can. (Plays havoc with the weight though!)

Remember, whatever you do, you are not selling, just collecting people for your reservoir. They may not use your service for ages, but if you keep in touch with them in a way that adds value without being too promotional, they will either buy spontaneously or recommend someone who will.

Make it Easy

The sales part is this. While not being overly promotional, don't on the other hand make it difficult or even impossible for people to buy your services when they are ready to do so.

Make sure you have contact details and they work. Make sure that people know your prices and don't have to ask (it's embarrassing for them). Educate them so that they know how to be your ideal client and feel privileged to be so. Let them know - and thank them - how wonderful it feels when they recommend you or refer someone into your reservoir (unlike my other hairdresser client who used to tell all her existing clients how busy she was, so they felt unable to recommend new clients to her).

Doing What Works

Finally, write down your plan and evaluate it monthly. Keep doing what works and drop what doesn't - unless you enjoy it! Not everything works in obvious ways. Decide on your preferred marketing methods and become the best at those methods. Educate yourself on how to be most effective, or hire a coach who can help.

And remember, 50% of all money spent on advertising is wasted, it's just that no-one knows which half!

Nicola Cairncross

Carole Spiers

Motivational Speaker,
BBC Broadcaster and Author

Carole doesn't just talk success, she lives it! Author of Tolley's *'Managing Stress in the Workplace'* and *'Turn Your Passion Into Profit'*, Carole is the founder of an international stress management group which has won repeat business for over 20 years with leading corporations from Unilever to Walt Disney, and Panasonic to the Bank of England. Carole is President of the London chapter of the Professional Speakers Association and a VP of the International Stress Management Association.

t: +44 (0)20 8954 1593
e: info@carolespiers.com
w: www.carolespiers.com

Chapter 7

Succeed on a Shoestring

Developing Success in One of the Worlds Toughest Environments

Carole Spiers

For many years I have devoted large parts of my life to helping people throughout the world, who for whatever reason have found it difficult to help themselves. And for the last three years, my partner and I have been revealing the inner secrets of self-marketing to budding entrepreneurs in the townships of South Africa's Western Cape.

The townships rarely get a good press, and the popular Soweto day tour is seen as a fashionable dare, rather than a desirable travel experience. But away from the big townships, often scarred with the kind of ugliness that tends to breed violence, you will find many small communities that are blossoming into useful life, and that reach out to welcome groups of discerning tourists. The craft villages of the Western Cape show this kind of enterprise at its best, and there is no doubt that a day or two in these scenic hills make a refreshing contrast to the more conventional delights of Cape Town.

Our first journey to Cape Town was made on New Year's Day 2005, from where we journeyed eastwards along the famed Garden Route. Since that time we now stay in a guesthouse and work in the townships at least twice a year.

Our initial aim was to go outside the usual tourist trail to meet the indigenous people of the region, i.e. the ordinary working African man and woman and, in particular, those who were running - or wanted to run - micro businesses. Currently it is still novel for overseas visitors to move away from the established tourist itinerary and also a little unusual for professionals from abroad to give time to local communities on a voluntary basis.

As our base, we chose the small seaside town of Mossel Bay. The focus of our first trip was to become familiar with the geography and a little of the history of the Cape and surrounding districts, and to learn something of the local economy and the interaction between its communities - black, white and Cape coloured.

During our second trip we embarked on a dialogue with members of the African community living in the townships of both Cape Town and Mossel Bay. We were also introduced to Anthea Rossouw, CEO of the Dreamcatcher Foundation - www.dreamcatcher.co.za - an organisation headquartered in Cape Town and with branches overseas, whose mission is to help and motivate South African entrepreneurs (and small business start-ups) to succeed by offering support, training and professional assistance. Dreamcatcher also encourage volunteers from all over the world to stay and work together with local communities on a variety of projects, and we found an immediate affinity and empathy with both Dreamcatcher and its passionate, dynamic, articulate and highly experienced chief executive.

The first step on the journey

Our third trip was pre-planned together with Anthea, and involved holding two-day workshops on Marketing Skills for Small Enterprises and Business Start-ups. The inspirational and motivational sessions, entitled *'The 8 Step Process to Leadership and Success: Empowering the Hidden Entrepreneur Within'* were held in Khayelitsha township in Cape Town, and taught the basic skills necessary to become leaders and entrepreneurs.

The attendees increased their understanding of what it takes to be successful in terms of commitment, determination and passion. In particular they:

- developed their self awareness in terms of their weaknesses and strengths and how these can be used to their benefit
- improved their personal and business communication skills so that they could communicate freely with potential customers
- spent time developing their image and learning what would help them stand out from the crowd
- learnt the importance of being professional and ensuring that this image was how they would become known
- learnt to understand that they themselves are part of the product they would be selling

The many attendees who came from various locations, some many miles distant, were enthusiastic and eager to learn the basic skills necessary for marketing their products or services and dealing with their customers. Although from different occupations and a wide age range, they all without exception were eager and enthusiastic to acquire new skills to improve their small businesses, and the basic skills of communication and marketing in order to start new enterprises.

One quality in all of them, however, stood head and shoulders above the rest – a resilience that enabled them to strive to rise above the difficulties in obtaining finance to fund their ideas and invest in their chosen business ventures. They believed in themselves and their ability to 'be someone'. This obvious trait made our experience of the training one of immense satisfaction, knowing that everyone attending the courses was so keen to better themselves. In fact, in all my years of training, I had never seen such commitment, motivation and determination from a single group of people.

As for the attendees, none had attended such a training programme before and they grabbed the opportunity with both hands. Their thirst for learning and knowledge made the atmosphere in the classroom electric. They wanted to be self-sufficient - not dependent on the State - and were determined they would succeed. These are just some of the things they had to say about their experience of the programme:

> *'The course helped me to stay positive no matter what the situation is or may be...'*

> *'I have learnt how to begin my dreams...'*

> *'Thank you for giving me the tools I need to start building my future...'*

> *'The course made me into the person I thought I could never be...'*

> *'The course opened my mind and brought light to my future...'*

> *'The programme gave me new life...'*

No Media Coverage Here!

If people with challenging backgrounds can look to the future with such admirable optimism in the face of such adversity, should we not be able to throw off the shackles of our self-limiting beliefs and pursue our own goals with renewed confidence? I for one know we can certainly do so!

It is both a privilege and an honour to be a part of my township friends' journeys to success. If by having a small role in their lives, I can develop their confidence and self-esteem, and provide the professional marketing skills that they need to become self-sufficient, then I am thrilled and delighted to be this catalyst.

There are too many times when we dash from one place to another: another plane, another train, another email, another meeting, another hotel; and sometimes along the way we forget some of the fundamental skills that we can pass onto others that can make an enormous difference for them.

There is no razzamatazz in the townships. There are no lights of the speaker platform, no BBC cameras - this is a behind the scenes activity! And it could not possibly be more different to the work I do in the buzzy fast pace of Dubai!

But when I come back from a working trip with my township friends, I come back with a feeling of respect, admiration and warmth, and a huge sense of satisfaction.

In my opinion there can be nothing more special in the world than making a difference to someone else's life, and then seeing that person make a difference to others. But one has to seek out these experiences – they don't just turn up on our doorsteps. We have to seek them, and despite the frenetic world we live in, they are still there to be discovered!

**Proven Formulas for Marketing Success
on next page**

Proven Formulas for Marketing Success

Do you wish you were better than you are?

Do you:

- Sometimes think that you are greater than the sum of your parts?
- Know you should be doing more to improve your life?
- Wish you could make a greater difference to yourself and those around you?
- Want to access your hidden potential?
- Learn by the mistakes of others or insist on making your own?
- Give as much energy to your dreams as you do to your fears?
- Think that 'success' is only for others?
- Lack confidence and self esteem?

The answers to all these questions lie within your grasp. You have as much right to be successful, to achieve your goals and to realise your dreams as the next person. It is all down to **you** designing your life and creating your own opportunities rather than letting life dictate them for you.

Do you find yourself saying 'success is for others but not for me' or 'other people have all the luck', as if luck were only dished out to a few? Have you chosen the 'opt-out' clause in your contract with life and feel fully justified in having done so?

Why do you do this? Is it because you think you don't deserve success? Is it because you would like to raise your game but simply don't know how? Is it because you think you don't have the ability to achieve? Or is it because **you** are getting in the way of your own success?

Your self-limiting beliefs and fears may be stopping you achieving your life plan. But believe me, you really can be:

- the BEST in your business...
- the BEST in your family....
- the BEST in your team...
- the BEST in your relationships...

You are the only obstacle to your success!

As soon as you acknowledge this you have the key to your success. You can begin to move on and start looking at what you have to do to make a positive difference in your life and be the success you deserve to be.

Passion isn't everything!

People think passion is everything. Well sadly they are wrong. 'Passion' and 'wanting success' are **not** enough to make it happen - which is why I need to let you into the secrets of what is:

- You don't 'achieve' success – you have to 'find' it.
- Success isn't about just doing – it's about making an impact.
- As Arthur Ashe, the Tennis Player said, *'Success is a journey and not a destination'.*

Passion is only the fuel. To succeed you need to assemble the engine - in the form of a **strategy** that will achieve sustainable, profitable growth. And doing this means concentrating on five fundamentals - my personal five-point plan for promoting you decisively to the next stage of your career:

Resourceful Entrepreneur's Guide to Business in the 21st Century

1. **Focus**

   - Know exactly where you want to go. Identify your goal and chart your route.

   - Research your market to ensure a favourable positioning of your product.

   - Write a formal Business and Marketing Plan including detailed costs and forecasts.

   - Maintain an attitude of total commitment and never allow yourself to get sidetracked.

2. **Prepare**

   - Think 'New Me' - a fresh mindset and an optimistic spirit of improvement.

   - Be ready for the sense of working in a different size or shape of team.

   - Let go of established routines that may not fit your new set-up.

   - Ditch any self-limiting beliefs that may have been holding you back.

3. **Develop your relationships**

   - Sustainable success depends on much help and inspiration by others.

   - Exploit every relationship you can - some of which may take years to mature.

   - Identify individuals whose skills will help you raise your game.

   - Join networking groups, cultivate gurus, hire a coach for key agendas.

4.   Promote yourself

- Create and broadcast a memorable image for yourself and your product or service.

- Take every opportunity to appear in the press, on radio and TV.

- Post your own publicity on the net, including prestigious White Papers.

- Use the net to bring in instant business via blogs, eBooks, CDs etc.

5.   Build your resilience

- Persistence is widely identified as the No.1 factor in business success.

- It's going to be a long trek – so don't be thrown by unforeseen setbacks.

- Don't let the pressure undermine your health. Eat, exercise and sleep well.

- Aim at total absorption in your work, in the spirit of loving craftsmanship.

Achieving success is a long and often challenging journey. But if you can keep these five fundamentals fresh in your mind, the one thing I can guarantee you is that it will be fruitful, and most of all it will be FUN! You have the power to make the impossible become possible – and your dream become your reality!

Carole Spiers

Toby Buckle

Combining many years experience of leading with the best of NLP, Toby focuses on leaders and individuals delivering authentic behavioural changes that have a high impact on performance. Toby has coached and trained personnel from across the UK and Europe.

Before setting up Hazelbranch Toby was in senior management at a large recruitment organisation that appeared annually in the top ten of the prestigious 'Times Top 100 Companies To Work For' awards and received the award for 'Best Training and Development Work'

t: +44 (0)7970 809594
e: toby@hazelbranch.co.uk
w: www.hazelbranch.co.uk

Chapter 8

Remain True to Yourself

The Authentic Article

Toby Buckle

Authentic seems to have become a bit of a buzz word recently. Many articles and books are written on how authentic leadership is required, authentic interactions are encouraged and authentic entrepreneurship is promoted in the form of social enterprise.

It is often hard to pinpoint exactly what being authentic means... Is it simply being more open about how you feel? Is it holding steady to a core set of values? Is it going with the flow and being spontaneous or being strongly aligned to a vision? Or is it recognising we are part of a bigger whole.

I believe being authentic means being comfortable with what you are doing and saying. From an NLP perspective this kinaesthetic alignment or congruency is a sure test when making decisions or statements. This sense of congruency is also the point where your inner voice isn't questioning what you say or do.

The sense of being authentic is a highly personal perspective and involves being true to your personal beliefs and values rather than copying styles of others. In terms of leadership I agree with Sydney Pollack in that "Real leadership probably has more to do with recognising your own uniqueness than it does with identifying your similarities."

For me personally, being authentic means not being overly polite (but not being rude), it means being self deprecating and feeling comfortable to joke. It also means being truthful about what others are doing or saying and what you think about it. It means acknowledging the events and experiences that have shaped my sense of identity and my beliefs and values.

There is also an element of being authentic which ties in with self-actualisation. Maslow defined the self-actualising life as "transcending self," as having "peak experience" moments when we sense the larger world, and the world of meaning. Being authentic is not self-absorbed or self-serving.

So am I being authentic?

Well I probably spent a lot of the last 20 years not being authentic.

At university I studied management science and took a module which looked existentially at life and the nature of work. The lecturers had slipped it in under the title work and society. The reading list consisted of such classics as Zen and the Art of Motorcycle Maintenance.

The whole relevance and meaning of accepting your role in corporate life was questioned. This had a profound impact on my belief that I shouldn't be just doing a job, but doing one I believed in and loved. However, for many years after leaving university I lacked courage and inspiration to find it. I was also driven by a notion that I needed to have money!

Like so many others I have drifted into jobs through lack of inspiration of what I would love to do.

In hindsight a goal setting experience or coaching session would have been useful. Teenagers deciding on university, first jobs or vocational training are often left to decide in an unstructured way, influenced by parent, friends and schools. A more values based method of deciding on what you want from life and work could be a better basis for careers advising. This might allow more people to find a path to self-actualisation or being authentic earlier.

For me the set up of the organisations I worked for which aimed to simply maximise profit at the expense of other goals, was out of line with some of my core values. As I climbed the ladder I was able to help run the business in a different way, putting time and effort into community initiatives, aiming to engage people in an intelligent and engaging way and found that in doing this I was engaged myself. For me this is the nature of self actualisation and being an authentic leader. When circumstances changed and new bosses imposed a more transactional philosophy I stopped believing the things I had to say and became inauthentic. Although I enjoyed the people I worked with and was good at the job I did, I still held an idea I was not supposed to be doing it.

To actually step away from the corporate life and the security and money that it paid took a series of events. Following a management course which focused on goal setting and coaching I set myself a goal of being a coach and I enrolled on an NLP course and found I loved it. It ticked the learning and developing boxes and gave me a vision of what I wanted to be. I started to coach and train people more in the company I worked for and in time became viewed as the company coaching expert.

It still took a reasonable length of time for me to break the conditioning and get out of my comfort zone of working for a company. As is common it took major life events to make me really push for a change.

My brother died whilst I was studying my practitioner level NLP, which again raised questions about the nature of reality and what I was doing. However, I had set myself a clear aim of being a director – mainly to prove to others I could do it. I reached that goal and for two years I stuck it out not realising time was slipping by, but then my mother died of a stroke out of the blue at a young 65.

I was in the middle of doing my master practitioner NLP – I finished the course went back to work and handed my notice in. I had missed out on seeing my mum as the nature of my job meant I was too busy to talk, make time to see her. I was determined that things would change and I would pursue the work I loved which was coaching and training others.

Over time I have considered the appeal of various strands such as career coaching, sports NLP, life coaching and business coaching. Being specific about which market to target is drummed into you at every 'how to market your business seminar' attended, however I have found my journey into coaching has meant my focus has evolved over time.

So am I now authentic?

The answer is yes, at least more often than I was.

When I am developing business now by networking or discussing what I can do with potential clients I now check in with my values and gut feeling as to whether I am being authentic and is it appropriate to be open, fallible and honest about what I do rather than trying to work out what the potential client wants to hear. It is tempting when meeting people to exaggerate what you have done and what you were or what you can do in the belief that it will encourage confidence in your ability and win you the business. It is worth taking a step back and asking yourself "Is this being authentic?"

I chose to work with organisations where I feel I can make a difference and I agree with their approach to working and ethical outlook. I also believe a new paradigm is needed in the way organisations in general are run and that innovation and engagement are key.

In this respect I agree with Bob Terry's definition of Authentic Leadership: Authenticity is knowing, and acting on, what is true and real inside yourself, your team and your organisation AND knowing and acting on what is true and real in the world. It is not enough to 'walk one's talk' if one is headed or leading one's organisation, community or nation, off a cliff!

Two further events have helped me become even more focused on what would be self actualising and authentic for me.

Eighteen months ago my first daughter Georgia was born. She was born disabled with a rare muscular condition. All the support and help we received made me realise that I wanted to be involved with giving something back in a bigger sense. I now also get involved with work with charities and social enterprises and looking at the broader nature of work and society which has rounded out the experience and sense of meaning I have in doing my work.

I also hired a coach. I read an article in Resource by Mary Lunnen. After reading Mary's article I felt a connection with regards to the questions raised around: Have your experiences given you insights? Would bringing more of you, the real you, into your work benefit your clients. Having come through my own series of personal challenges these were questions that particularly rang true for me and prompted me to contact Mary. Following that we have embarked on a series of coaching sessions which have helped realign my motivation and reset some goals in developing my own business and I began to get a really good idea of where and what to focus on and had the confidence to become authentic.

I have built this into the leadership training I do in encouraging people to take the mask off and work out what sort of leader they want to be. If I'm feeling daring I point out it is OK sometimes to be vulnerable, open or just exasperated!

So what have I learnt?

I have learnt that it is easy to fall into the belief that we should have the skills and abilities to guide ourselves and cope with all life throws at us. What I have now realised is stopping to think about what we want out of life on a regular basis, paying someone to help do this is time and money well spent, no matter how good you are at coaching others. Being a coach is sometimes being like the plumber who never fixes his own leaky tap. You know what you should be doing and yet you don't make time to do it.

Most importantly I have learnt that my experiences as a whole make me who I am. It is important to think about how your experiences have shaped and influenced your current sense of you and that enables you to be authentic and perhaps self-actualising. It is not always appropriate to give our life history however when communicating, if I am able to be more natural and authentic it is possible this will develop deeper connections.

I'm finally being myself a bit more rather than too eager to please or put on a front of being something I'm not. I'm being authentic more of the time and it feels better.

Toby Buckle

Richard White

Richard White is a sales coach and trainer for IT Consultants. He specialises in winning more sales from business networking and is the author of 'The Accidental Salesman - Networking Survival Guide'.

Richard is also the founder of TheAccidentalSalesman.com which provides free online sales training for people who hate selling.

w: www.theaccidentalsalesman.com

Chapter 9

Attract Clients Naturally

You don't Need a Personality Transplant to be Good at Sales

Richard White

You have fulfilled a longstanding ambition and started your own business. You have decided to leave paid employment for a life of independence and eventual affluence. Congratulations! You now have a career in sales! Every month thousands of people stumble into sales by default by starting a business and then go on to struggle to consistently generate enough sales for themselves. If they are lucky they lurch from feast to famine and back again!

I actually got into sales by accident myself, just over ten years ago. I became the head of a business unit within a medium sized consultancy. It did not take me long to realise the job was predominantly a sales role. Like so many people who start a business, I hated the idea of selling. I was a professional not a salesman! My saving grace was my ambition. I was determined to cling onto my significantly expanded salary and my dreams of one day running my own consulting practice.

I was excited when I came across NLP and specifically the modelling aspect. I invested in my own NLP training and set about building a model of excellence for selling IT consultancy. I created it just for myself and called it 'Soft Selling' for want of a better name. I was looking for a style that helped me succeed in sales without feeling like I was selling or that my clients felt like they were being sold to.

I needed to be sure I would gain and maintain the trust and respect of my prospects and clients as an expert rather than being seen as a pushy sales person. I also needed for the approach to be backed up by a solid and measurable process based on sound sales principles. Sounds like a tall order!

It took me three years to go from hating selling to loving it and outselling most of my colleagues. I never felt like I was selling when with clients but the reality was that I never stopped! The wonderful thing is my clients loved my style and would often do the selling for me!. Over time I realised that the key to my Soft Selling system was not the techniques but the mindset behind the techniques. When I started studying top sales people in other industries I was surprised to find that they actually shared a similar mindset even though the process and techniques were different.

So how do you develop the confidence to sell without a personality transplant? I thought I would share some of the insights I have gained along the way. Unfortunately there is not one silver bullet or pearl of wisdom that will magically turn you into a fearless red meat-eating sales person. Adopting each insight, however, will give a significant boost to your confidence and collectively they will provide you with all the sales you need.

Insight 1 - Become a student of sales

In order to master anything you need to become a student. When you decide that you are committed to becoming confident and competent with sales then you become open to learning. You need to develop your own style that works for you and that is why reading and learning is important. Just fifteen minutes study a day adds up to 7.5 hours a month. That's a whole day! If you don't have time to read then buy some audio books and listen to them in the car or when you are doing the chores around the house. You should also give yourself feedback and review your performance and seek to be making small improvements all the time rather than big gestures.

Insight 2 - Seek different perspectives

Did you ever experience seeing a spectacular view on a sunny day? Then you go back on a day when the sky is grey and the rain in falling hard. You are in exactly the same place and yet get a totally different outlook. The way we look at things changes the way we perceive them. If we want to understand how to best think about sales then learn to see things in the same way as someone whose abilities and values you admire. The best way is through some form of mentoring relationship but just by seeking new perspectives we will begin to find them.

Insight 3 - Learn how to motivate yourself

Activity is everything in sales and motivation drives activity. I like to think of it as 'motive for action'. Having clearly defined and motivational goals is a start. You need to have them for the long term as well as the shorter term. If your goals do not excite you into action then get some that do! As well as clearly defined goals make sure you have a roadmap for achieving the goals. This will ultimately break down into sales activity. Your goals do not have to be materialistic at all but they do need to be compelling enough to drive you forward.

Insight 4 - Work on your fears and limitations

Whenever you do something new then it is a little uncomfortable. Yet the more you do something the more you get used to it. If motivation is the accelerator in a car then fears and limitations are the brake. These include the way you handle rejection and failure. If you approach the sale in the right way you will never be rejected and you will never fail either!

Insight 5 – Work on your people skills

People do business with people they know like and trust. Professionals typically are introverts to some extent and their people skills can be further developed. Although personal development will reduce levels of shyness and increase self confidence, it will not change an introvert into an extrovert. That's not a problem in sales, especially if you want to sell to executives. Where having the 'gift of the gab' can actually be a disadvantage.

Insight 6 – Get good at discovering the motivation to buy

Developing self-confidence, excellent people skills and high levels of motivation is all very well but if you do not have what people want to buy then you are going to have a hard job in sales! If you assume that people do not buy products or services for no reason at all then you need to discover the motivation to buy. There are only two primary motivators – pain and pleasure. Pleasure in sales is about the prospect moving towards something desirable. Pain is about moving away from something undesirable. Often the potential buyer wants both! I discovered that it was much easier for people to justify spending money to move away from something they do not want. In the current status quo and I made it my business to find a target audience where I had credibility and they had real unresolved pain.

Insight 7 – Learn to tell stories

If there is one skill that will help you to sell without feeling like you are selling it is storytelling. All the top sales people do it naturally and you can learn to do it too. People who like each other trade anecdotes and talk in stories. If you incorporate storytelling into your style then you will find everything so much easier! You can use stories in so many different ways in sales. For example, when you first meet someone ask them their story of how they started in business. It really helps to break the ice much better than any rapport technique I know. Have your own stories about how you started in business and how you have helped clients to successfully resolve their problems. You can also develop stories to inoculate against objections and to up-sell other products and services.

Insight 8 - Clarify your sales process

What really surprised me and surprises lots on accidental sales people is that selling is not just one activity but a whole series of activities. Each business will have a natural process of taking a sale from initial interest to cash in the bank. It should be a repeatable process that others could follow if necessary. Getting clarity about the specific actions required to achieve the desired level of sales gives a huge boost in confidence.

Insight 9 - Do lots of activity!

There is a saying that selling is a numbers game. It's actually an activity game. I like to think of the sales process as a sausage machine. One of those old fashioned ones with a big handle on the side. You put the meat in the top and turn the handle and the sausages drop out the end in a line. The point here is that unless you keep feeding the machine and turning the handle then sausages will stop coming out the end! Plenty of activity helps you notice what works and where your machine can be fine tuned.

Insight 10 - Hold yourself accountable

If you have a boss that understands sales management then they will be working with you to stay motivated and coaching you to raise your game and meet your agreed targets. They will also hold you accountable for achieving those targets. If you don't have someone to keep you focused on the activity and your targets then it is easily slip into the 'feast or famine' syndrome. This is where an external sales coach can pay huge dividends. If you don't like the thought of a sales coach then see them as a personal sales manager.

You owe it to yourself and your family to master sales. You **can** sell without compromising your integrity or damaging relationships. You will not change the way you feel about selling overnight but it will happen relatively quickly if you embrace sales and work at it.

Happy selling!

Richard White

Bill O'Hanlon

Bill O'Hanlon is a dynamic, inspirational professional speaker and prolific author (30 books so far) who helps motivate people and organizations to determine what they are meant to be doing and to remove the barriers to succeeding at those goals.

Originally trained as a psychotherapist, Bill became known for his collaborative respectful approach, irreverent humour, storytelling, clear and accessible presentation style and his infectious enthusiasm for whatever he is doing. He teaches seminars, leads trainings, writes books, coaches people and offers websites, podcasts, blogs, web-based courses, tele-classes and audio and video programs. Bill is often invited as a keynote speaker, conference speaker, motivational keynote presenter and business speaker.

e: bill@billohanlon.com
w: www.billohanlon.com

Chapter 10

Position Yourself Expertly

**There's a Book in You -
and it will have to come out**

Bill O'Hanlon

"I think I'd like to write a book".....

**You don't know how many times I have heard that in my 25+ years
of teaching workshops. Want to guess how many of those people
actually wrote their books? A very small percentage, I can assure
you.**

Why is there such a slip between cup and lip when it comes to writing
the book you know you have in you and that would really contribute
to the world?

A few years ago, I began coaching people about how to write, how to
write well, how to organize and focus their book projects, and how to
successfully navigate the confusing and sometimes frustrating world
of publishing. I have just completed my 23rd book and having been

published by large mainstream publishers (Penguin; HarperCollins; W.W. Norton; Rodale), smaller professional publishers (Guilford; Brunner/Mazel), as well as having self-published both in print and over the internet. I have learned through hard-won experience how to both write books and get them published.

Here is a list of typical reasons people give me about why they haven't written their books (yet, I often add):

I don't have enough time

Why should I bother to write it; it will never get published?

I don't have anything original to say

It's arrogant to think I could write a book

I can't put myself out in front of people (this is a popular one in the UK; for some reason, I never seem to hear this one in the U.S.)

I can't write; I'm no good at it

I'm disorganized; hyperactive; like to talk better than I like to write; and so on

What I write must be perfect and I must know every reference and everything about my subject before I write the book

I'll never be as good or as smart as [fill in the name of the writer you are comparing yourself to here]

I am sure some of you reading this can fill in your own reason, but suffice it to say they all have one thing in common. They are things you say to yourself or think that don't help get the book written.

Here is the Zen of writing:
The only way to get a book written is to write it.

Everything else is commentary and reasons. One successful writer, when asked how he writes so much, gives this simple explanation: *Bum glue! I glue my bum to the chair and write.*

Obviously it is not so easy for many people, even after hearing such enlightening and clear advice. That is why I created a seminar for helping people get their books written and published. After having a mission to transform psychotherapy and feeling it is coming to completion, I thought I might be able to stay home and rest a bit, but I found another passion had seized me: I love to help people figure out what their contributions are and remove the barriers to realizing those contributions. Since I think there are many of you who have books that would really help the world and other people, I am committed to helping you clarify what the book is about, get it written and get it published.

Below there are some tips which will help you with those beliefs and ideas that might poison your writing dreams and goals.

The Poisons That Will Kill Your Writing Dreams and Ambitions (and Some Recommended Antidotes)

1.   The Perfection Poison

The conditions must be perfect; My information or knowledge must be complete and perfect; My writing skills must be perfect; I must read another book about writing or go to another writer's course or workshop . . .before I start or do a project.

Antidotes:

- *Isabel Allende once taught a class on novel writing and suggested her students try to write the "Worst American Novel." Try to write badly. Do a bad first draft, giving yourself permission for it to be bad and wrong.*

- *Use a computer instead of writing freehand, It is easier to erase, cut and paste.*

- *Start writing. Most good writing is rewriting anyway.*

2. The "I don't have anything original to say" Poison

It's all been said before. Everyone knows this already. I don't have anything important to say. Nobody will want to read it. Who the Hell am I to think I have anything to say or that I can write a book?

Antidotes:

- *You have a unique slant/way of saying it. Trust that.*

- *Find your writer's voice.*

3. The "I don't have time to write" Poison

I have to make money, raise kids, have responsibilities, am too tired, am too busy, will write someday when things slow down or I go half-time, or slot out one day a week for my writing

Antidotes:

- *Bulls---!*

- *Maya Angelou tells of writing her early books with her children crawling all over her in the kitchen. There are orange juice and vomit stains on some of her early manuscripts.*

- *Steven King wrote his first novels while working full time as a janitor.*

- *I wrote my first ten books in ten years with four kids at home with a full time job.*

4. **The "This will never get published, so why bother to write it" Poison**

So many people have unpublished novels in their drawers. The publishing industry is so competitive. I don't know how to get anything published. I tried and was rejected by all the publishers/agents/magazines I tried. I'll fail.

Antidotes:

- *Only God knows the future and what will get published. Lest you get confused, remember you are not God.*

- *Get some coaching and/or more information about how to make it more likely your stuff will be published. Then try again. "Ever try? Ever Fail? No matter. Try again. Fail again. Fail Better." - Samuel Beckett*

- *The publishing industry needs product to keep functioning. Publishers are constantly looking for publishable books and the next big thing.*

5. **The "I'm not in the mood to write/I'm not inspired" Poison**

If I sit down to write when I am not inspired or visited by the Muse, the writing won't be good, so why bother?

Antidotes:

- *Then do corrections, formatting, outlining, backups of your material or research during this non-inspired time.*

- *"Sit down and write. It will take care of all those moods you're having." - Ray Bradbury*

- *"Inspiration comes during work," says author Madeleine L'Engle, "not before it."*

- *Write anyway to exercise your writing muscle, so that when the Muse deigns to visit, you'll be ready with your writing skills intact and well-developed.*

6.   The Comparison Poison

I don't have as big a platform, as _____

Antidotes:

- *Go to the bookstores and see how many books are published that aren't that great or that have been written by people you've never heard of.*

- *Model on them or find your own unique strengths or ways of compensating for your weaknesses.*

And we'll give the last word to Somerset Maugham:

> *"There are three rules for writing the novel. Unfortunately, no one knows what they are.*

Bill O'Hanlon

Andy Smith

An Emotional Intelligence coach based in Manchester, UK. He has been running the Create the Life You Want workshop (now incorporated into the four-day NLP Foundation Skills course) for the last 10 years.

His company, Coaching Leaders Ltd, runs NLP Practitioner and Master Practitioner courses in Manchester, and provides Emotional Intelligence coaching, assessment and training to organisations. Andy's corporate client list includes Sony, Mintel, BP, Roche, The Cabinet Office, the NHS, and Lancashire County Council.

t: +44 (0)7967 591 313
e: andy@coachingleaders.co.uk
w: www.coachingleaders.co.uk

You can order Andy's book, Achieve Your Goals: Strategies To Transform Your Life (Dorling Kindersley 2006). from the following website

w: www.coachingleaders.co.uk

ISBN 978-1-405315-86-9

Chapter 11
Plan Well

Three Pitfalls of Goal Setting - and how to Avoid Them

Andy Smith

When you begin a new venture, and as you continue to develop in your business and life, it's important to think at least once a year about how you want to change your life, to set goals for the future, and to make commitments. In previous years, even when you have gone through the essential steps of stating your goals positively, been specific about what you want, and set a date by which you want to achieve them, there may have been times when they just didn't happen. The chances are that they fell foul of one or more common mistakes in goal-setting. Andy Smith, author of *Achieve Your Goals: Strategies to Transform Your Life* (Dorling Kindersley), identifies these traps and how to make sure you don't fall into them.

Pitfall No. 1:

Not taking into account the knock-on effects of achieving your goal

The ancient saying "Be careful what you ask for, in case you get it" is a very wise one. Because your unconscious mind will do its best to give you what you ask for – no more, no less – you have to be very clear about what the goal is that you are setting.

Consider a businessman who very single-mindedly sets a SMART goal of owning a company with a turnover of a million in its first year.

A year later he has his company which has turned over a million, so he has achieved his goal. But – his health is shot due to working 19-hour days, he's a hundred pounds overweight because he's been living on junk food, his wife has left him because he's never home, and he has no friends left because he has made deals with them that left him with a big profit and them with very little.

This is not where he wanted to be, but because he did not consider the consequences and knock-on effects, his unconscious mind gave him exactly what he asked for – and no more.

How could he have avoided this? As well as making the goal sensory-specific and putting a date on it, he also could have looked at the consequences of achieving the goal on every other area of his life:

- his health
- his family
- his friendships
- the wider community

If you don't consider all the consequences of your goal, you may end up with something you don't want. The smarter way to set goals is to take the consequences into account, allowing you to make changes to your goal and/or your route to achieving it. That way you stand a chance of gettingg the benefits of your goal while avoiding unwanted side effects.

Bonus tip: listen to your unconscious mind

The conscious mind can only track around seven "chunks" of information at a time (less on a bad day) so it's easy to miss something vital when you are thinking your goal through.

Your unconscious mind, by contrast, is potentially aware of everything, and it can notice pitfalls that your conscious mind overlooks. One of the ways it communicates with the conscious mind is by means of feelings. So - check how you feel when you think about your goal. Do you feel enthused and energized, or tired and discouraged?

If you feel less than 100% about your goal, that may indicate that your conscious mind has missed something about the consequences of achieving it, so check again.

Pitfall No. 2:

"Taking too much on" and getting discouraged

It can be very easy to set a big, compelling goal – and then feel overwhelmed by the effort you think it will take to get there. The goal is so big, and so different from how things are now, that getting there by the deadline you have set will surely demand too much of you. And the more you think about the legwork it will take, the more discouraged you feel.

There are two things you have to do to regain your motivation.

Firstly, when you think about your goal, picture how wonderful it will be when you have achieved it, rather than what you will have to do to get there. This will instantly feel more motivating. When you book a holiday or a weekend away, you are thinking about what you will do when you get there - not about traffic jams or delays at the airport.

Secondly, break the goal down into smaller sub-tasks that feel easier to achieve. Make each of these tasks a goal in itself. This means that you can feel good when you achieve each one - maybe even give yourself a reward.

Sometimes it isn't easy to see what you should be doing first. The smart way to decide on the sub-tasks that will form your route to the goal is to start from imagining the position of having achieved the goal already. From that perspective, ask yourself:

"What conditions had to be in place in order for this goal to be able to happen?"

Ask the same question for each of these conditions – and so on, working backwards through time until you arrive at the very first step you have to take. This gives you your route to the goal (or routes as there may be more than one way to get there).

If the first task still seems overwhelming, break it down into smaller tasks until the first step is one that you can definitely, no question, accomplish.

Remember what management guru Peter Drucker said:

"We overestimate what we can accomplish in one year, but we underestimate what we can accomplish in five."

The key is to get started.

Pitfall No. 3:

Not Knowing What You Want

This is the biggest and most common goal-setting mistake of all - not getting round to setting any goals because you don't know what you want.

You can be an expert in all the goal-setting techniques known to man, but if you haven't taken the time to find out what you really want, one of two things is bound to happen:

You don't set any goals. This means that you drift, and life just happens to you, and you have to react to whatever it decides to throw at you. This might work out OK if you're lucky - and it might not.

(It's perfectly possible to drift in a well-paid corporate career, by the way – for the first twelve years of my working life, I sleepwalked through my IT career and was quite comfortably off by the end of it. But because I had no direction, I was unfulfilled and also vulnerable to career upsets.)

You set goals because you think you should, or because someone else tells you to but they are not really about what you want. You don't achieve your goals, because your unconscious mind sabotages them, or you achieve them but discover they are not what you really wanted. Either way, you still feel unfulfilled.

So how, in Carlos Castaneda's words, do you choose *"a path with heart?"* How do you find your calling?

You can use either or both of these methods:

Method 1

Take some time to discover your values in each area of your life – for example, what's important to you in a career? What's important to you in a relationship? Elicit the values for each area in turn by asking just that question:

"What's important to you?"

You will get the best results when you get a friend to ask you this question, especially if they keep asking even after you think you have found all your values. Some of the deepest and most motivating of your values will be the ones that you are not at first consciously aware of.

Some values are more important to you than others, so decide which are the 'must-haves' and which are the 'nice-to-haves' - and then go for fulfilling all of them anyway!

Method 2

Try out as many different experiences as you can. Notice what you enjoy (or don't enjoy) about them? What is it about each experience that you really liked? Which of your values was it calling to?

The more reference experiences you have, the clearer idea you will have of your preferences, boundaries, and the 'hot buttons' that really excite your motivation; ultimately, the more idea you will have of who you really are.

Conclusion

When you have made the necessary adjustments to your goal to take into account knock-on effects, to make sure that it is appropriately 'chunked', and above all to make sure that it reflects what you really want at the deepest level, don't be surprised if you feel a renewed surge of motivation! As you take action to make your goals happen, remember to take a moment every week or so to check that you are still on track, and to scan the horizon for any new factors that might require you to make adjustments to your course. And when you do achieve your goal, remember to give yourself credit – after all, you've earned it!

Andy Smith

Robyn Pearce

A CSP (Certified Speaking Professional)
Robyn is the Time Queen. She mastered her own time challenges and now helps people around the world overcome theirs. She can show you how to transform your time challenges into high productivity and the life balance you desire. She works regularly in the UK, travelling from her base in New Zealand.

Download her free report "How to Master Time", a simple yet powerful diagnostic tool to help you identify your key areas for action. You'll find it at www.gettingagrip. com/products/e-books/index.asp And while you're there, enrol for your free Top Time Tips – practical advice every two weeks

t: +64 9 232 0523
e: robyn@gettingagrip.com
w: www.gettingagrip.com

Reference:
www.sleepingchinese.com

Chapter 12

Get Things Done

In Order To Go Faster,
First We Must Go Slower

Robyn Pearce

How often do you go into an energy slump in the early afternoon and find yourself thinking, 'I'd love to shut my eyes for a wee nap'? Do you follow your body's direction - or do you follow society's expectations and stick at your desk?

If the latter is your normal experience, do any of the following experiences sound familiar as you endeavour to push through that 'tired' space?

You've been working normally at a keyboard but suddenly there are lots of typos or other errors.

Your normal level of energy has just flown out the window. You realise you're feeling exhausted, sometimes quite suddenly.

You might be yawning.

You're working at about quarter speed.

Concentration is a challenge; you find yourself re-reading information you would normally scan and comprehend swiftly.

You notice you're thirsty, hungry or uncomfortable in some other physical way.

And when such symptoms occur you've probably also noticed that it takes at least 20 – 30 minutes for the energy flow to return, the pace to pick up again and your 'second wind' to kick in.

While all this is going on, you might look around at your colleagues (if you work with others), assume they're working at full efficiency and feel guilty about your 'slack' time.

Here's the thing – the desire for a nap in the early afternoon is normal. But countless people, especially Westerners from cooler climates, have been socialised since the Industrial Age to ignore the messages their bodies try to give them.

It's time for those of us in industrialised and North European-style business communities (including those in the Southern Hemisphere such as Australia and New Zealand) to rethink this habit. I believe we need to take a lesson from the smart folk in the warmer Mediterranean countries (with their restorative afternoon siestas) and also the Chinese. Did you know that it's normal practice in China for people to nap at their workplaces, including corporate offices, after lunch? (Check out www.sleepingchinese.com)

I know a number of very efficient Western business people who often take a short nap in the early afternoon. 20 minutes is all we need to recharge. In that time our brain slows down to the alpha state, very similar to meditation. Any longer and we'll probably drop into a deeper sleep – this won't give the same kind of benefit. Awaking after 15 – 20 minutes we might feel a little dozy for a couple of minutes but then we're up and away again – operating at top efficiency for the rest of the day. And not only more efficient, but also, having taken a break, many of us are more creative.

Resourceful Entrepreneur's Guide to Business in the 21st Century

In my role as an international time management specialist I work with people from all around the world. They're from almost every industry - lawyers, accountants, financial planners, bankers, educators, other professional speakers and subject matter specialists like myself, CEOs and senior managers of a wide range of industries, health professionals, farmers, and many owner/operators and staff of small to medium businesses. Because 'sanity breaks' are part of my message I almost always ask my audiences if they take a regular lunch break, and how many take tea breaks — not just the 'grab a cuppa and take it back to the desk' kind of tea break, but a real one where they give their brain a rest — away from their desk. Typically more than 70% of the room, many of them knowledge workers, tell me they don't do either on a regular basis.

The next questions are 'how effective are you in the afternoon?' and 'how tired are you at the end of the day?' The look on people's faces is classic — a kind of bemused 'why didn't I notice that connection before?'

Here's the explanation. Various biological rhythms flow through our body all day, all night. Ultradian rhythms are just one sort. Loosely translated ultra = many and dian = day — the many rhythms of the day. They cycle continuously through our body like rolling waves — 90–120 minutes up; 20 minutes down.

The down cycle is *not* a negative thing — instead it's the rest cycle that our body needs in order to recharge, rebuild and to grow. If we keep pushing through these down cycles, if we don't give our body a chance to recharge, we push the poor old thing into flight or fight. The consequence? You already know. Stress, burnout, and eventually sickness. Without exception, every person I've challenged on this has agreed that when they push through those down cycles of tiredness, thinking perhaps that they're being lazy or that it's not appropriate to slow down for a short while, they become less effective in the afternoon and end up dragging their weary bodies home at the end of the day – not much use to themselves or loving family waiting for their share of time.

It's also a fatigue management and safety issue. We see messages about fatigue on our roads – but the same message should also be shouted in the workplace. Many of the worst accidents we've seen in recent times have occurred at the end of long shifts - Chernobyl being just one example.

The problem is, our society is becoming sleep-deprived. Almost all of us are awake for longer hours than a century ago, due to the opportunities afforded by electricity. Add to that the impact of an increasing global economy and the advent of the internet and modern telecommunications; since the 1980s many people have an increasing sleep deficit. How many people do you know who never turn off their BlackBerries or other PDAs? Or take their laptops home almost every night so they can continue to work? Or they work across borders and have to get up early or stay up late to talk to colleagues or clients on other sides of the world?

So what to do about it?

Morning and afternoon tea breaks and a lunch break away from your desk – they're some of the simple solutions. It's surprising how many professionals don't now take breaks any longer than a few minutes. They go to the toilet, make a hot drink and head straight back to their computers. They *think* they're being efficient by working through both tea breaks and lunch. Wrong thinking!

Let's go back to power naps as a strategy. That's what kept Winston Churchill operating at full steam through all those tough war years. When tired he'd pop upstairs (when he was working at Downing Street) and hop into bed for about 20 minutes. He also had a special nap chair near his office. A few of the other famous names who applied

Resourceful Entrepreneur's Guide to Business in the 21st Century

the same habit - Margaret Thatcher, John F. Kennedy, Beethoven, Benjamin Franklin, Leonardo Da Vinci, Eleanor Roosevelt, Johannes Brahms, John D. Rockefeller, Dali, Robert Louis Stevenson and Albert Einstein.

Have you noticed that the best ideas never come when you're sitting at your desk? And how often is a brilliant idea or the solution to a problem sitting in your mind when you wake in the morning. Imagine tapping into that resource through the day. Often it is when we nap that fresh ideas, new insights, and solutions rise to the surface of our mind. According to the Salk Institute for Biological Studies (http://www.salk.edu/index.php) naps enable our brain activity to remain high throughout the day. If we fail to take a nap, our brain activity declines.

Einstein knew this. He was very deliberate in his use of power naps, using them to solve problems. He would relax in a comfortable chair or on a sofa, his head propped on his hand whilst holding a handful of ball bearings. When the hand relaxed enough to drop the ball bearings he would wake up and quickly write down whatever was in his mind. Many of his most brilliant ideas came to him in this alpha state or twilight zone. He relied on the noise of the falling ball bearings to wake him up; to have slept longer would have taken him into deep sleep.

'But I work in a corporate environment and can't take a nap', you might be saying. Really? If you take the time to notice the messages your body sends you, and if you can show your employer or colleagues the benefits they reap from your increased effectiveness in the afternoon, you might be surprised how much support you get. If employers realise they'll get higher productivity and less mistakes, why wouldn't they support such behaviour?

Maybe you don't have the luxury of a door. Look for other solutions such as going to your car in the car park, maybe a sick room or perhaps there's a quiet room you can use.

Nike is just one of a number of large corporations who now provide quiet rooms (or relaxation rooms) which their employees can use as they choose (as long as there's no talking). Other companies make it 'ok' for staff to leave their desks to refresh and revitalise. After all, that's what smokers do several times a day, every day! (But no, I'm not suggesting we all go back to smoking!)

And now, I'm off for a 'creative moment'. Happy napping!

Robyn Pearce

For a summary of 12 research projects from around the world that discuss the efficacy of napping see:

www.metronaps.com.au/australia_files/benefits/studies-and-research.aspx

Lisa Wynn

Lisa is a Profit and Prosperity Coach and works across the world with individuals, businesses and corporations to create lucrative, fulfilling work. Her seminars are upbeat and fun and her approach to prosperity both practical and spiritual. She is an Accredited Master Coach (ECI) and a Professional Certified Coach (ICF) as well as a qualified Wealth Creation Coach.

w: www.corporatepotential.com

Chapter 13

Know Your Numbers

What's Your Financial IQ?

Are you Financially Intelligent or in need of a Money Makeover

Lisa Wynn

A recent Egg survey found that the overall understanding of money and finances in the UK is worryingly low with the average score on their test being 56 out of a possible 120.

Even accountants (the highest scorers) only got 90%!

A mere 1% scored full marks whilst 3% got 0!!!

To my mind and experience a less surprising result was that people have strong emotional responses to money. This was only touched on to a small degree in the survey, but they described "financial shortsightedness" as a grave problem for Britons' finances.

Here are some of Britain's other financial habits:

- 78% of Britons say they are too busy to check their finances regularly

- 33% have been charged four times or more in the last year for exceeding limits on accounts

- People spend on average 10 minutes a week looking at their finances – women spend more time than men

- Only one in every three under-30s is putting money aside for their old age

The government is seriously concerned about our financial bad habits and are issuing strict warnings and playing with the economy to try and stop us spending. However, according to the Motley Fool financial website:

- At the end of January 2011 Britons owed a record £1.45 trillion pounds – that's £1,450,000 million.

- Our total debt has increased every single month for the last 141 months – at the rate of about £8-10 billion a month!

- As a nation we spend 110% of our monthly income.

On the reverse side of the coin one of the fundamental financial behaviours that mean that an individual is most likely to achieve their financial goals are very simple – probably the top of this list is tracking one's income and expenditure.

Remember – there are only three financial behaviours you can have:

- Earn more than you spend

- Spend what you earn

- Spend more than you earn!

The trick is to move towards the first of these and then further and further into that state of being around money.

Sounds simple!

So why are the dire warnings and even the constant fear of debt that so many are living in not having an impact on our spending behaviours?

The answer I believe lies in the fact that our behaviours are actually only a symptom of our beliefs and attitudes to money. Those attitudes and beliefs actually drive our behaviours – when we try and change at a behavioural level we are fundamentally dependent on self discipline – and let's face it, if we had a ton of that we wouldn't be a trillion pounds in the red!

So how would you describe your Money Mind? Are you financially "well adjusted" or "an emotional wreck" when it comes to finances? The best way to tell is almost certainly to take a look at your financial wellbeing. If you are saving well (over 10% of your income), investing wisely and feel confident about the future, then your Money Mind is on your side.

If - as many of the people I meet in seminars and individual coaching find – you get dizzy at the thought of even looking at your bank statements; if you don't know what you are worth financially; if your credit cards don't get cleared monthly then you are in need of a Money Makeover.

What are some of the steps then to a Money Makeover?

Choose change:

As Confucius said "If we do not change direction, we will end up where we are heading"! Make a decision now to be differently, to act differently and to be open to having things differently.

Many people approach me wanting to change their life through changing their financial status but they are half hearted and reluctant to be different around money. They may feel they have chosen wealth – but they aren't prepared to make changes to get there.

Understand your Money Mind:

Our relationship with money is fundamental to our financial wellbeing. Take a moment now and imagine that Money is a person. How would you describe your relationship with other?

- Are you friends? Enemies? Distant acquaintances? Long lost relatives? Strangers?

- How do you feel when you imagine that Money is coming to visit?

- What is your picture of Money when it arrives?

In asking these questions of ourselves, we are delving below the conscious mind and looking at the deeper drivers and beliefs that we hold about money. Without knowing these, it is hard to change our behaviours because they are driven from a deep, subconscious desire to stay the same.

Write yourself a "Letter from Money":

Sit down and write yourself a letter from Money. Let Money tell you just how it feels about your relationship and how you treat each other.

- What does Money want from you?

- For you?

- How is it prepared to work with you from now on?

- What advice does Money have for you?

Really relax and let your imagination flow.

- What behaviours does Money believe will help you best?
- What's the one thing that if you were to do it, everything would start to flow better?

Capture it all in the letter and keep it safe!

Understand your value system:

Values can be a major clash area for wealth creation activities and consistently turn out to be the major block in people's healthy behaviours. Our values represent what is most important to us and yet few people ever stop to think what they are.

The consequences of being unconscious about these values is that when an action appears to our subconscious mind to be contradictory to our values, it just shuts down. Our inner self says "No, shan't!" we have an inner tantrum and it shows up as procrastination or inability to make a decision on what to do next – or even what we really want in life.

Write down a list of everything that is more important to you than money.

Then ask yourself: How could having more money positively influence this?

So, if health is more important to you then money, how can having more money impact your health for the better? In this, you are looking at your drivers, but also creating motivation.

If the most important things in life are not to your mind affected by money, then it will be very hard to create enough energy to take consistent, focussed action. Money needs to feel important to you before it would want to come and visit!

To have more money you must fundamentally shift your Money Mind!

Lisa Wynn

Steve Nobel

Steve worked in international banking for 10 years before becoming a director of Alternatives, a non-profit organisation based in the heart of London.

Steve is a writer, trainer and workshop presenter and coach.

w: www.stevenobel.com

References:

Lynn Twist: *The Soul of Money:* Sept 2003

W.W. Norton & Company Ltd.

ISBN: 978-0-393050-97-4

Chapter 14

Understand True Wealth

Freeing the Spirit of Money

Steve Nobel

*Did you know that the world's 200 richest individuals
own as much as the combined yearly income of the world's
poorest 2.5 billion people?*

*And that we currently spend over
$1000 billion globally on military budgets.*

In my own life money has been a huge challenge; there have been
times where I have felt I did not have enough of it, or when it was
there I did not always enjoy the work I did to earn it. I worked in the
city in banking for ten years where I saw lots of wealth and millions
of pounds being transferred around the globe daily. I later worked in
local government in the Housing directorate for ten years and came
to witness considerable poverty and deprivation. My third career
change came after a lot of personal development seminars and
spiritual workshops when I eventually found myself being a director
of a well-known organisation in London that promotes holistic talks
and workshops on a wide range of topics.

If I could sum up my experiences and beliefs around money in one sentence it would be this - that our thinking around money determines whether we have a positive or negative experience with it. I believe this to be true at both a personal level and at a global level. I am not asking you to believe this with me but I offer here a few ideas around money that you might want to consider. For instance there is a wonderful book that I highly recommend by Lynne Twist called *The Soul of Money* where she describes the three toxic myths that underpin our global thinking around money.

Toxic Myth One:

There's Not Enough - this says not everyone can make it and that some people will be sidelined and left out. Here there is not enough food, water, housing, time, jobs and money. Here the focus is always on not losing.

Toxic Myth Two:

More is Better - with the fear that there is not enough comes the great drive to acquire more. This fuels a fierce competition for seemingly scarce resources and is a race with no real winners only losers. Even those who have vast resources often live unfulfilled and fearful lives. This idea has for centuries eroded the natural sustainable abundance of the planet.

Toxic Myth Three:

That's Just the Way it Is - says that although it may not seem fair we had better learn to play the game. This contains considerable hopelessness and resignation yet still manages to create tremendous resistance to change. It has long allowed much corruption and greed to run unchecked on the planet.

These myths have created over time a fear based kind of thinking I call poverty consciousness that believes in: competition, greed, hard work and no play; lack and scarcity; sacrifice and struggle; fear and manipulation; hoarding and squandering; winning and losing; taking from the others; survival of the fittest; and that conflict and warfare are the best means to solve problems.

Please do not despair because it is always possible to unplug from the fearful matrix and become prosperity adventurers. Here you begin to buy into a very different paradigm of thinking where you become a little wiser and smarter around money.

*'If you are going to let the fear of poverty govern
your life ...your reward will be that you
eat but you will not live.'*

George Bernard Shaw

It is my belief and experience that money is attracted to those who have healthy beliefs about it and is repelled by those who feel desperate or fearful around it. For instance I have met many well-meaning people who believe in spiritual values or in social justice who just cannot seem to do well with money. I have also had the good fortune to meet a few millionaires who create great good and amazing opportunities for those around them.

On the other hand I have known many 'poor' people who felt so victimised around money that they spread a lot of gloom, hopelessness and misery wherever they go. Of course many rich people are also locked into poverty consciousness and constantly worry about losing their assets, and there are many people, particularly in poorer countries, who have few possessions yet possess an abundance of love, laughter and generosity of spirit. Although having money is no guarantee of happiness, money does offer more possibilities for making a positive difference in the world.

Here are six ideas about money that could transform your world.

1. *Money is more than a medium of exchange, it is energy that can flow or stagnate.*

2. *Money as energy is attracted, directed, moved and repelled by our ideas, our beliefs and state of being.*

3. *Money as energy is attracted by vision, passion and purposeful action.*

4. *Money as energy is repelled by fear, desperation and blame.*

5. *Money as energy stagnates through grasping, greed, and hoarding.*

6. *To create abundance money must circulate and flow through positive intent and deed.*

Every one of us has inner resources such as love, creativity, knowledge, freedom, and some sense, however vague, of vision and purpose. It is just that some of us are better at putting these resources to work than others. Nelson Mandela led his country away from civil strife because of an inspiring vision.

Richard Branson created an inspiring business brand through his own determination and passion. We all have access to outer resources such as money, relationships, training, information, mentors, teachers, coaches, property, and so on. Some of us have found and adopted better strategies for building and nurturing our inner and outer resources than others. It is always possible to learn new and smarter strategies to live more prosperously. On the next two pages are six suggestions you might want to consider that could change your relationship with money.

Tips to Change your Relationship with Money

1. **Examine and Change your Limiting Beliefs and Judgements.** What limiting messages did you receive about money from your family? What unhelpful messages did you receive about money whilst passing through the education system or at work? Examine all your beliefs and see which ones you have adopted without question. Look at your judgements for they will form unseen barriers to you allowing in more money. Do you judge rich people as being arrogant, selfish or uncaring? If so why would you want to become well off?

2. **Create Higher Values Around Having Money.** Create a set of values around having and spending money. Values such as generosity, gratitude, integrity and joy would change the way you relate with money. What would happen if you chose to earn, save and spend your money more ethically? What about choosing to earn money through ways that work for your upliftment and others? It is possible to earn money from doing the things you love.

3. **Release Any Desperation.** There is the paradox that when we feel desperate about our survival then we keep money away. Practise stopping worrying about your bills and instead focus on appreciating what you have. Bless your debts and the people that trust in you to repay them. Bless all the money you spend and appreciate what you receive in return. Open to having money come into your life from many different avenues. Are you willing to receive money from unexpected avenues?

4. **Affirm Abundance. How much do you feel you are worth? Do you feel you deserve to have all your needs and wants met in the world? Affirm that money can be a source of good in your life and in other people's. Everyone is born with the potential to be abundant regardless of upbringing. Take off any limiting price tag you may have placed on yourself. Take steps to having the real things that you want without waiting for cash to make it happen**

5. **Give Generously. Practise one small act of generosity each day. A smile or a word of appreciation costs nothing. We can only receive from others what we are willing to give. Give generously to yourself and spend some of your money on what makes your heart sing. Trust that what goes around eventually comes around and expect to receive from some unexpected and unusual places.**

6. **Practice Stewardship rather than Ownership. Nothing in your life truly belongs to you; everything is on loan during this lifetime. We can take nothing material with us. Stewardship is a much lighter way to travel than ownership. See everything as being on loan from the universe.**

Steve Nobel

Chapter 15

First Things First: Back to the Beginning

Christine Miller

"The reasonable man adapts himself to the world; the unreasonable one persists in trying to adapt the world to himself. Therefore, all progress depends on the unreasonable man."

George Bernard Shaw, Maxims for Revolutionists

It may seem a little odd to end this book with a beginning, but after all, we are entrepreneurs, and we don't do things in conventional or even in reasonable ways! Therefore in a delightful paradox, in order to *close* I am going to offer you the opportunity to *open yourself* – to start over and re-evaluate why you are in business, and what it is you stand for, so that you can shine as an icon in the crowded marketplace. It's all about *your* story and *your* uniqueness, what sets you apart from the crowd, yet what unites you with the world, (another neat paradox) and what will ultimately contribute not only to your success but to creating beneficial change on a much larger scale.

In the foregoing chapters you've met some compelling characters with their own inspiring stories, delivering powerful advice; and you will have picked up plenty of ideas to help you become a resourceful entrepreneur. None of this will make any difference, though, unless you take some action and make the right things happen so you get into the flow of productive habits that bring you clients who want (and love) your products and services.

Back at the beginning, in Chapter One, are eight criteria for being a Resourceful Entrepreneur, (which you can also find on the www. resourcefulentrepreneur.com website), and some questions to ask yourself about why you are *really* in business: or, if you are just getting started, ask yourself why you're going into business in the first place. If you haven't completed them yet, I'd suggest you make that the next thing you do when you've finished reading this chapter.

I often hear from people that they had lost sight of the passion and enthusiasm that inspired them to start their business, the changes they dreamed of instigating, and the service they had envisioned performing, because they'd got so bogged down in the day to day necessities that the fun and joy had disappeared. That big shining vision of transforming the world and helping people had dimmed. Giving themselves the time and space to develop their answers to the eight Resourceful Entrepreneur criteria fires up their energy again and they feel more alive to what they want to achieve.

They welcome the opportunity to stop for a while and reflect on the early days, reconnect with the true purpose of what they do, and simply take some time out to be still and think, perhaps supplemented by attending an event or talking with a mentor or coach who helps deliver a different perspective.

One *'make a difference'* resourceful entrepreneur, Karin Ridgers of Mad Promotions and VeggieVision, told me:

> *"No one tells you how challenging the journey is when you want to be an entrepreneur – how caught up you get on doing the business when you must also need to work ON the business.*

Taking time out is vital for your growth and events and courses that help you think about why you went into starting your own business can be inspiring. When I read your Resourceful Entrepreneur workshop information, the workshop I want to be at NOW, Christine, the 8 criteria all really hit home and the questions that you also noted made me stop and think. **Who am I doing this for? Who can help me?** *Sometimes you just work flat out and do not stop to "sharpen the blade" as such!!!*

The workshop is a welcome breather away from the workload to take time. Think about what the entrepreneur really wants and for me as a participant to re-connect with why I wanted to set up in the first place. **At the moment I don't remember!!!!"**

Karin's story is typical of a busy entrepreneur who loses touch with their purpose and vision, their Story - the original big 'Why?' and needs some support in re-discovering the vitality essential to keep moving forward.

What's Your Story?

Tell a Compelling Story

In the process of establishing the 'Why, Who, What' of your business you can begin to develop your 'story', what it is that is unique and irresistible about your brand. Because rest assured, even if it is only you, as a solopreneur, or a partnership or boutique business - you *do* have a brand, and that brand is built on who you are and the impression you make on the people you come into contact with. Even if you are a well-established business, it's a good idea to revisit your 'story' regularly and add any elements that might have changed with your development and the results you are creating. How do you tell your story so that it is a true and compelling representation of who you are and what you do, why you do it, and what your contribution is, so you're understood and believable?

Your Offering

Three Factors to Draw Out the Essence

What? What? How?

Ask the questions below about your business and make sure your answers are simple and understandable to someone outside your industry or profession: whether you're planning to go for funding, need to explain your offering to a potential client or capitalise effectively on a PR opportunity with the media, having a strong message will make a big difference to your successful results.

- **What is it you're doing?**
- **What do you want to be known for?**
- **How do you want people to feel about you and your business?**

Make sure the answers you arrive at here are reflected in everything you do, so that you give a consistent message and are unmistakably authentic. This will bring you clarity and will counter the main problems faced by new (and established) businesses seeking to be accepted and recognised as solution providers for their clients. If you really drill down and get to the essence this will help you be consistent in the identity you convey, everywhere you go. It will also help you identify potential partners and collaborators to co-create with.

When we build, let us think that we build forever.
John Ruskin

Your Marketplace

The Three 'W's Process to Pinpoint Your Positioning

Who? Who? What?

These questions relate to your marketplace, your target audience of clients. Consider:

- **Who** - the group they belong to – your niche or target
- **Who** - what they want – here you appeal to their needs and emotional wants
- **What** - what they get – here you present yourself as the solution to their problem

Your answer might be something like the example below which is the 'who, who, what' of a client of ours who offers recruitment services to financial professionals looking for more meaningful careers:

"Who" We help leaders in the financial world

"Who" (What they want) - who are seeking meaningful roles with ethical organisations

"What" (what they get) - learn how to find and obtain and excel in their ideal position.

"We enable leaders seeking meaningful roles with ethical organisations to prepare, perform and profit from successful career transition."

Work on your message until you 'have it' and own it in a way that you are both convinced and convincing, and you'll find it stands you in good stead wherever you go. You can incorporate it into your 'presence' – in your brand message with your marketing materials. You'll have a ready and sincere answer when someone asks what you do, and when you're very clear on your target audience, you'll find you spot opportunities and matches for your goods and services in places you wouldn't otherwise have noticed.

Your Focus

As a resourceful entrepreneur another great benefit of knowing your market and having your purpose and message clearly articulated is that you can very quickly bring yourself back to focus and action when you slip into the doldrums if things haven't gone entirely as planned. It enables you to see the longer term possibilities, and treat the unexpected as a lesson to be learned and moved on from quickly. We usually learn a lot from our mistakes because they force us to look for a different ways of proceeding, and as long as the bigger picture holds true we can pick ourselves up and overcome the challenges.

> *"Success is not measured by what you accomplish*
> *but by the opposition you have encountered, and*
> *the courage with which you have maintained*
> *the struggle against overwhelming odds."*
> Orison Swett Marden

Your Resourceful Mind

In addition to your focus, your persistence will also be required, and for this you'll need a resilient, resourceful mind-set which enables you to bounce back and continue through tough times. This doesn't mean you need to be unrealistic and Pollyanna-ish, but you do need to be able to see through and round problems without losing faith. Developing a resourceful mind and believing in your ability to overcome are definitely pre-requisites for entrepreneurs, and for that you need to take time out to reflect and have quiet time to build your own compelling sense of what the successful future for you and your business holds. That's not always easy for energetic entrepreneurs on the go, but it is an important part of being balanced in business and life.

> *"The gem cannot be polished without friction,*
> *nor man perfected without trials."*
> Chinese proverb

Another valuable but underrated aspect of your resourceful mind is the power of your intuition or gut feelings. How often have you ignored that little voice that tells you not to do something, or encourages you to go ahead, and lived to regret not taking the guidance? I think we all have those experiences, and entrepreneurs are more likely than many to tune into their natural instincts and flair and follow their gut. You can develop your intuitive skills by observing the results of decisions you make and checking them for effectiveness and success. It doesn't mean blindly following every thought that comes into your head, and it's wise to check ideas against a feasibility and practicality scale rather than blithely assuming they will work untested.

It's an advantage of learning to be in a calm and resourceful state that your intuitions become more attuned to the solutions you are seeking, as your brain works more creatively to supply you with brilliant ideas from the unlimited bank of innovation. Whole mind thinking is very powerful and is the fuel behind great thinkers and inventors through the ages such as Leonardo da Vinci, Kekulé, Einstein and Edison.

"The rational mind is a faithful servant, the intuitive mind a divine gift; the paradox of modern life is that we have begun to worship the servant and defile the divine."
Albert Einstein

Your Consistency

Your consistency is about doing what you say you'll do – and more; *even going beyond what you say you will do, just for the joy of it.* We all have times when we might not meet expectations for exceptional reasons, but in the usual course of business life, keeping promises and going that bit further to delight your clients makes a big difference to your success. Firms and brands that consistently rate highly with customers are renowned for ensuring the customer experience is exceptional, and such organisations are rewarded with repeat business and a sound reputation.

So that you can deliver above and beyond expectations as your business develops, think about what you might need to do to ensure smooth running, and consider outsourcing as soon as you possibly can. Delegate, collaborate, seek joint ventures, mastermind and brainstorm for new ideas, and make sure you are consistent in the way you take care of yourself – without the driving force of your underlying entrepreneurial passion, your business won't get very much further!

"Only if you reach the boundary will the boundary recede before you. And if you don't, if you confine your efforts, the boundary will shrink to accommodate itself to your efforts. And you can only expand your capacities by working to the very limit."
Hugh Nibley

Let Them Know You Care

As you make your way along the road to success, you are going to need and want a lot of support. Let's be blunt here and call it Love. Not romantic 'love', though you will probably want that too, but the kind of Big 'Love' that is a way of being, which cares enough about you, and you about them, for it to be a source of wellbeing and stability in your life, yet which is not afraid of being tough when required.

You're going to want your clients to Love you and your offering; you're going to want any employees and business associates to Love you; you're really going to want a friend, mentor, partner, family member or other personal support resources to be there when you're facing tough decisions. And you're going to want them all to know you Love them, too.

The best way to receive is to give first, so make it a priority to have the best interests of others at heart, which may mean declining opportunities when they don't seem totally ethical, or where you can see unintended consequences of harm beyond profit or short term gains. It means not cutting corners, always being vigilant and alert to poor service or quality, rectifying faults as fast as possible, admitting mistakes, and keeping the bigger picture in focus.

In these days of transparency and openness you can't afford not to be caring, careful and scrupulous, because your audience is watching, all the time, and they are inclined to punish firms and people who don't meet their standards or who fudge about issues such as sustainability and responsibility.

In personal terms, make Love a strength, turn it into a power in your life by demonstrating how caring and compassion transform the entire business arena into a much more satisfying experience which rewards at every level, including the bottom line. It's not a soft option, in fact it's tougher to be truly caring and loving than to be indifferent and uncaring – but the dividends are long lasting and have been demonstrated in many organisations, including highly successful South West Airlines, who embrace a culture of 'Love' and have 'Luv' as their ticker on the New York Stock Exchange.

Now - Break the Rules

"Hell, there are no rules here -
we're trying to accomplish something."
Thomas Alva Edison

The simple truth is that for creative entrepreneurs on fire, there really are no 'rules'. Sir Richard Branson would tell you that when he started Virgin, he and the people around him ignored all conventional business procedures, because they simply didn't know what they were! They knew what they wanted to achieve and that they wanted to be different, but they really struck out with innovative ways of operating. And you too have an open platform to come up with different ideas, try out alternative solutions, bring in methods from completely different industries, and keeping experimenting until you find what works.

However, that all takes precious time – and time is not something anyone can afford to waste. So as a resourcefully clever entrepreneur, look for effective ways to achieve results fast. There are definitely some processes and ideas in The Resourceful Entrepreneur Experience that can speed things up for you; they are real, living, breathing, tried and tested ideas and practices that have worked for many, and can work for you.

*"Remember, you can earn more money,
but when time is spent it is gone forever."*
Zig Ziglar

Ultimately you will find your own ways of operating, and of succeeding. You don't have to be a particular type, dress in a certain fashion, or even have a specific kind of training – but you do need to be agile, persistent and confident in yourself, believing in your offering and your contribution to the world. Stretch yourself as far as you can go, and then go even further – you will be amazed what you can achieve as a resourceful entrepreneur. Push the boundaries – whilst you stay resourceful, be kind, listen carefully, keep the end result in mind – and remember that the world needs you.

***Entrepreneurs are the future, especially truly
resourceful ones like you, who can bring benefits
beyond measure to a challenged world.***

Christine Miller

*"Most of us can learn to live in perfect comfort on higher
levels of power. Everyone knows that on any given
day there are energies slumbering in him which the
incitements of that day do not call forth. Compared with
what we ought to be, we are only half awake.*

*It is evident that our organism has stored-up reserves
of energy that are ordinarily not called upon — deeper
and deeper strata of exposable material, ready for use
by anyone who probes so deep. The human individual
usually lives far within his limits."*

William James

Additional Resources

The contact details on the author pages in the book will direct you to resources specific to their work, where you will find some excellent complimentary material. We have also gathered a range of additional resources to help you further in your business, a selection is shown below.

Some are exclusive downloadable PDFs; others are online guides on external sites which may require you to give your email details. You can find them by visiting our website and registering for free membership which will allow you to receive updates about our ever-expanding **'rqbank'** of information.

- **'The Bootstrappers Bible' - Seth Godin**
- **'Guide to Business Blogging' – Debbie Weil**
- **'A Bookwright Guide to Killer Blogging' – from Tom Evans, 'The Bookwright'**
- **'Twitter Handbook' – Deborah Micek and Warren Whitlock**
- **'The Social Media Guide' - Matthew Tommasi**
- **'Top 12 Reasons Why Most People Fail to Attain their Objectives' – Christophe Poizat**
- **'Think Like an Entrepreneur Support Tools' – Robbie Steinhouse**
- **'The Magic Story – Recipe for Success' - Frederick Van Rensselaer Day**
- **'10 Key Strengths for Entrepreneurs' – Christine Miller**
- **'Ultimate ReSource Guide to PR' – Christine Miller**
- **'Ultimate ReSource Guide to Writing a Book Proposal' - Christine Miller**
- **'Your Ultimate ReSource' – a web portal dedicated to business and personal growth**

Information about subjects like social media and online networking is changing constantly, and we think it's more useful and timely for you to use the internet to research and refine your approach, which is why we didn't devote a chapter specifically to the topic. There are some good guides above which will set you on the right track.

www.resourcefulentrepreneur.com/rqbank
Go there NOW to download your complimentary business resources.

Other Publications

In this Series

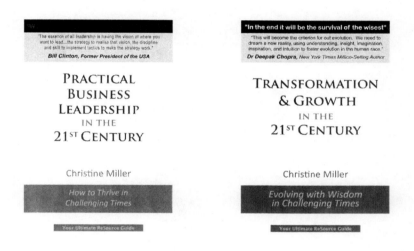

Coming Soon

Find out more about these and other books at
www.portopublishing.com

Lightning Source UK Ltd.
Milton Keynes UK
174793UK00001B/23/P